Proxy Voting of Pension Plan Equity Securities

Other publications of the
PENSION RESEARCH COUNCIL

Fundamentals of Private Pensions—Dan M. McGill
Concepts of Actuarial Soundness in Pension Plans—Dorrance C. Bronson
Social Aspects of Retirement—Otto Pollak
Positive Experiences in Retirement—Otto Pollak
Ensuring Medical Care for the Aged—Mortimer Spiegelman
Legal Protection of Private Pension Expectations—Edwin W. Patterson
Legal Status of Employee Benefit Rights under Private Pension Plans—Benjamin Aaron
Decision and Influence Processes in Private Pension Plans—James E. McNulty, Jr.
Fulfilling Pension Expectations—Dan M. McGill
Collectively Bargained Multi-Employer Pension Plans—Joseph J. Melone
Actuarial Aspects of Pension Security—William F. Marples
Status of Funding under Private Pension Plans—Frank L. Griffin, Jr. and Charles L. Trowbridge (out of print)
Guaranty Fund for Private Pension Obligations—Dan M. McGill
Preservation of Pension Benefit Rights—Dan M. McGill
Retirement Systems for Public Employees—Thomas P. Bleakney
Employer Guarantee of Pension Benefits—Dan M. McGill
Reciprocity among Private Multiemployer Pension Plans—Maurice E. McDonald
A New Look at Accounting for Pension Costs—William D. Hall and David L. Landsittel
Social Security and Private Pension Plans: Competitive or Complementary?—Dan M. McGill (ed.)
Pension Mathematics—Howard E. Winklevoss
Indexation of Pension and Other Benefits—Robert J. Myers
Joint Trust Pension Plans—Daniel F. McGinn
Financing the Civil Service Retirement System—Dan M. McGill (ed.)
Continuing Care Retirement Communities—Howard E. Winklevoss and Alwyn V. Powell
Social Investing—Dan M. McGill (ed.)
Employer Accounting for Pensions—E. L. Hicks and C. L. Trowbridge
Pensions, Economics and Public Policy—Richard A. Ippolito
Search for a National Retirement Income Policy—Jack L. VanDerhei (ed.)
Pension Asset Management: An International Perspective—Leslie Hannah (ed.)
The Economics of Pension Insurance—Richard A. Ippolito

Proxy Voting of Pension Plan Equity Securities

A compilation of papers presented at the 1988 Symposium for Institutional Members of the Pension Research Council of The Wharton School, University of Pennsylvania

Planned and Edited by
DAN M. McGILL
Wharton School of the University of Pennsylvania

Ralph H. Blanchard Memorial Endowment Series
Volume III

1989

Published for the
Pension Research Council
of the Wharton School

by

IRWIN

Homewood, IL 60430
Boston, MA 02116

Project editor: Paula M. Buschman
Production manager: Carma W. Fazio
Compositor: TCSystems, Inc.
Typeface: 10/12 Melior
Printer: R.R. Donnelley & Sons Company

Library of Congress Cataloging-in-Publication Data

McGill, Dan Mays.
Proxy voting of pension plan equity securities/planned and edited by Dan M. McGill.
p. cm.
Includes index.
ISBN 0-256-07645-6
1. Pension trusts—Law and legislation—United States. 2. Proxy—United States. I. Title.
KF3512.M335 1989
344.73'01252—dc19
[347.3041252] 89–1691
CIP

Printed in the United States of America
1 2 3 4 5 6 7 8 9 0 DO 6 5 4 3 2 1 0 9

PENSION RESEARCH COUNCIL

PURPOSE OF THE COUNCIL

The Pension Research Council was formed in 1952 to undertake academic research into those institutional arrangements designed to provide financial resources for a secure and dignified old age. It seeks to broaden public understanding of these complex arrangements through basic research into their social, economic, legal, actuarial, and financial foundations. While generally geared to the long view of the pension institution, projects undertaken by the Council are always relevant to real life concerns and frequently focus on issues under current debate. The Council does not speak with one voice and espouses no particular point of view. The members do share a general desire to encourage and strengthen private-sector approaches to old-age economic security, while recognizing the essential role of Social Security and other income-maintenance programs in the public sector.

Foreword

Employer sponsored retirement plans in the United States, including those of state and local governments, hold about $2.2 trillion in assets. Roughly 40 percent of these holdings, or almost $900 billion, is in the form of common stock. This represents about 23 percent of the market capitalization of all common stock issues listed on the organized stock exchanges in the United States and those traded in the over-the-counter market. Legal title to these equity securities must be held by duly designated trustees or life insurance companies licensed under the laws of more than one state, but they may be managed for investment purposes by banks, life insurance companies, registered investment advisors, or the plan sponsor (so-called in-house investment). The voting rights associated with this vast accumulation of corporate ownership place enormous potential for economic leverage in the hands of the parties entitled to exercise those rights. The dominant portion of this voting power is concentrated, at least nominally, in a relatively small number of very large financial institutions.

To explore the business, legal, and regulatory environment in which these voting rights are exercised, the Pension Research Council invited a group of recognized authorities to prepare papers on various aspects of the subject and present them at a symposium in May 1988, on the University of Pennsylvania campus. More specifically, the symposium focused on who has the legal right to vote the common stock in qualified pension (and profit-sharing) plans; the source of the voting authority; the fiduciary obligations attending the exercise or nonexercise of the voting rights; and the statutory, regulatory, and judicial standards against which the behavior of the various fiduciaries are judged.

Papers were presented on the fiduciary obligations of the basic types of fiduciaries under a qualified pension plan: the named fiduciary (representing the plan sponsor), the plan trustee, and the asset manager or managers, with emphasis on the fiducial implications of proxy voting of equity securities. These papers took as their point of departure the strictures of basic trust law, as modified and expanded by the Employee Retirement Income Security Act (ERISA), which were set forth in a comprehensive background paper prepared by Professor Norman Stein of the University of Alabama Law School. The fiduciary obligation of the plan sponsor in voting plan equity holdings was discussed by Robert Sandler of Reinhart, Boerner, Van Deuren, Norris & Rieselbach and Hazel A. Witte, Assistant General Counsel of the U.S. Small Business Administration, from a jointly prepared paper; the obligation of the plan trustee was expostulated by Larry Cagney of Debevoise and Plimpton; and the obligation of the asset manager was analyzed by Professor Alfred Conard of the University of Michigan Law School.

The proxy voting issue was then examined from the standpoint of organized labor, public sector plans, and the general public by Howard Young, now Adjunct Professor at the University of Michigan but formerly a senior staff member of UAW; Sarah Teslik, Executive Director of the Council of Institutional Investors; and David Walker, Assistant Secretary of Labor. The symposium discussions were summarized and critiqued by John Langbein, Max Pam Professor of American and Foreign Law, University of Chicago, his views on the general subject of proxy voting of pension plan assets being reflected in a paper subsequently prepared (at the editor's urging) for inclusion in this volume.

Subsequent to the symposium, George Cowles, Senior Vice President of Bankers Trust, a major institutional player in this arena, prepared a paper (again, in response to a plea from the editor) on the proxy voting process, including pass-through voting, under various fiducial relationships.

These papers constitute the subject matter of this volume. From them, collectively, one learns that, in a sense, the right to vote the common stock shares of a pension plan rests initially with the *named fiduciary*, generally a staff official or internal committee designated by the plan sponsor on formation of the plan. The named fiduciary, acting within the procedures established by the plan, appoints a trustee for the plan (or enters into a contractual arrangement with a life insurance company). In the absence of contrary instructions or arrangements, the trustee will not only hold legal title to all plan assets (an ERISA requirement) but will manage and control the assets and vote the shares of any common stock holdings. The plan documents may, however, give the named fiduciary the right to vote the equity securities of the plan. Furthermore, the plan document may permit or require the named fiduciary to designate investment managers to assume the trustee function of managing and controlling the assets of the plan, including the authority to vote the equity securities over which they exercise discretionary control. It is the prevailing practice for the entity that exercises investment discretion to vote the equity securities. Finally, under individual account plans, the plan participants may be permitted to vote (by pass-through procedures) the common stock shares allocated to their particular accounts, particularly when the stock is that of their employer.

The plan sponsor, having delegated the proxy voting right to some other entity or entities, may not properly instruct such other parties on how to vote the proxies.

When the equity securities of a pension plan are voted by an entity other than the trustee, the latter must still execute (sign and date) the proxy voting form since it holds legal title to the securities. The trustee sends the executed forms to the investment manager (or other proxy-voting entity), which returns the forms directly to the issuer or in some instances to the proxy solicitor.

There is a question whether the voting of proxies for pension plan common stock holdings is a mere ministerial function, without fiduciary significance, or the exercise of discretionary authority over plan assets. Some have maintained that proxy voting is a fiduciary act only if the issue that is the subject of the proxy voting has economic or financial implications. Others assert that the right to vote equity securities is inherently a valuable right and when held in respect of pension plan assets is, itself, a plan asset. Under the latter view, the entity that possesses discretionary authority over proxy voting is a plan fiduciary, and every exercise or nonexercise of that authority is a fiducial act.

There seems to be a consensus that the rules of classic trust law, so ably elucidated by Professor Stein, which were formulated over the years to define relationships and set standards of fiducial behavior under private gratuitous trusts, are ill-suited for the complex relationships that exist under a conventional pension plan. The modern pension plan is a multiparty contract for the mutual advantage of the plan sponsor and the plan participants, lacking many of the characteristics of a personal trust. Yet a number of basic common law rules for personal trusts were embodied in ERISA without modification. Professor Langbein calls this the "fallacy of the transposed category."

These scholarly papers, from which the foregoing sketchy observations were drawn, are a valuable addition to the growing literature on the fiduciary implications of proxy voting of pension plan equity securities. The Pension Research Council—and the entire pension community—is indebted to the authors for sharing their knowledge and time. The symposium was a real learning experience for all participants; it is unfortunate that the dialogue between members of the audience and the speakers could not be published in the proceedings. A significant step in that direction was taken by persuading George Cowles and John Langbein to reduce their informal commentaries into a form suitable for inclusion in the monograph.

It goes without saying that the views and opinions expressed in the book are those of the respective authors and are not necessarily shared by members of the Council.

Dan M. McGill

Contents

Proxy Voting of Pension Plan Equity Securities

CHAPTER 1

Trust Law and Pension Plans

by
Norman Stein*

The topic of this symposium is the fiduciary implications of proxy voting of pension plan assets. One might legitimately query why a symposium on such a subject should begin with a paper whose title alone disclaims any but a passing interest in proxy voting. The answer is simple: Professor McGill asked me to write this paper.

Professor McGill, however, had his reasons for wanting this paper, and they are good reasons. Pension law, both pre- and post-Employee Retirement Income Security Act (ERISA), is intimately connected to the law of trusts and its unsettled but nevertheless unforgiving geography of fiduciary obligation. Discussion of almost any substantive pension issue draws on trust concepts. Thus, we perhaps can forgive Professor McGill for wishing the symposium to commence from its basic point of reference, which is the law of trusts.

The purpose of this particular paper, then, is to provide background and context for the other papers. But Professor McGill has also encouraged me to offer my views on the symposium topic wherever appropriate, and I am of course delighted to have the opportunity, although I must confess at the outset that my view is only that the question of how pension managers should cast their proxies has many dimensions and no clear answer.

The paper has five substantive sections. The first section introduces the trust and briefly traces its origins. The second section identifies and discusses basic trust concepts that may have applicability to pension plan trusts. The third section considers ERISA's adoption, and modifi-

* Associate Professor, University of Alabama Law School.

cation, of trust concepts. The fourth section summarizes some of the difficulties with applying trust principles to pension plans. The final section introduces the topic of the symposium, proxy voting.

AN INTRODUCTION TO TRUST AND FIDUCIARY CONCEPTS

The trust is a juridical invention anchored in a notion of property that permits bifurcation of the property's possessory and beneficial ownership. In other words, the trust permits one person or persons to possess, and thus manage, property for the benefit of others. Put another way, the trust permits an owner of property to dispose separately of the burdens and benefits of that property.

A detailed history of the trust, and its singular contribution to Anglo-American property law, is not possible here (and probably not desirable). We might note, however, that our trust concepts began to emerge in medieval England, where division of the beneficial and legal incidents of ownership through a trust permitted property owners to evade the burdens and restrictions that feudal law placed on the ownership of land.[1] In some senses, then, the early development of the trust can be credited to precisely the same impulse that today inspires people to consult tax attorneys.[2]

In the beginning, creation of a trust depended on trust, the trust placed in the individuals to whom legal ownership of property was transferred, for the medieval British law courts were reluctant to fashion equitable remedies for beneficiaries defrauded of their property interest. A beneficiary denied relief by the law courts had recourse only to the Crown, which by the 13th century had come to refer such requests for relief to the Chancellor and, ultimately, to the Court of Chancery.[3]

The Court of Chancery of this period dispensed with the inflexibility of the law courts and instead dispensed equity.[4] This meant that in the case of trusts, the trustee would be ordered to fulfill the responsibilities he had accepted. Ultimately the Chancery Courts developed a body of trust law that explicitly recognized a fiduciary relationship between the trustee and beneficiary that relied upon equitable princi-

---

[1] More detailed histories of the trust can be found in G. Bogert & G. Bogert, *The Law of Trusts and Trustees* (2nd ed., 1984), Chapter 1, and in Fratcher, *Scott on Trusts* (4th ed., 1987) § 1.

[2] The felicity of observation is not mine; I first heard it in a class lecture by Professor Bertel Sparks at Duke University Law School.

[3] G. Bogert & G. Bogert, *The Law of Trusts and Trustees* § 3 (2nd ed., 1984).

[4] As historians of Anglo legal history, and readers of Dickens's *Bleak House* know, the arteries of Chancery ultimately hardened.

ples to settle disputes between them. In fact, it would only be slightly misleading to characterize trust law as a series of particularized applications of the general demands our legal system places on fiduciaries.

Treatises of great volume are devoted to sorting out those demands, but Justice Cardozo, in a passage that will be familiar to most lawyers, condensed those demands into a set of aphorisms in a 1928 judicial opinion. The passage is worth quoting:

> Many forms of conduct permissible in a workaday world for those acting at arm's length, are forbidden to those bound by fiduciary ties. A trustee is held to something stricter than the morals of the market place. Not honesty alone, but the punctilio of an honor the most sensitive, is then the standard of behavior. As to this there has developed a tradition that is unbending and inveterate. Uncompromising rigidity has been the attitude of courts of equity. . . . Only thus has the level of conduct for fiduciaries been kept at a level higher than that trodden by the crowd.[5]

TRUST CONCEPTS AND PENSION PLANS

This section of the paper describes specific trust concepts and principles that, at least in theory, were directly or indirectly applicable to trusteed pension plans before enactment of ERISA. Some initial reflections on trust law and pension plans might provide a helpful introduction for the reader.

Before ERISA, the term *pension law* was perhaps something of a misnomer, since it described not laws about pensions but rather a web of trust, contract, insurance, labor, and tax laws. The reason was that pensions were legal entities generally in the form of a trust, based on contractual underpinnings, and sometimes regulated by the government when they impinged on management-labor relations or the tax laws. When disputes arose, courts identified the appropriate substantive area of law and then purported to apply the rules of that area to the problem at hand. Thus, if the dispute were a trust dispute, the law would draw on trust concepts; if the dispute were understood as contractual, the law would draw on contract concepts.[6] It is probably safe to say that disputes sometimes implicated trust law. It also is probably safe to say that the trust law questions might be categorized as questions concerning relationships: the relationship of the trustee to the trust property, the relationship of the trustee to the beneficiary, the

---

[5] Meinhard v. Salmon, 249 N.Y. 458, 464, 164 N.E. 545, 546 (1928).

[6] *See, e.g.,* Hunter v. Sparling, 197 P.2d 807 (Cal. 1948).

relationship of both the beneficiary and the trustee to third parties, and finally, the continuing relationship of the trust settlor to the trust corpus and the other trust parties.

Pension law, then, was sometimes merely the application of trust law to a particular kind of trust. In a seminal article to appear in the 1988 volume of the *University of Chicago Law Review,* Professors Langbein and Fischel argue that trust law at times has proved an unsatisfactory, even perverse, framework for ordering the legal relationships of parties to a pension plan.[7] Langbein and Fischel observe that trust law developed in the context of judicial resolution of disputes in private trusts, where relationships between the parties are relatively simple. In their view, the application of certain trust principles to the more complex, multiparty relationships in pension plans sometimes yields rules that run counter to the economic realities that should govern those relationships. This is an important perspective for this conference, since to the extent we are making policy judgments about proxy voting by pension managers, we should consider in the first instance proxy voting in an economic, and perhaps social, framework, and, only after reaching our conclusions, should turn to the trust law concepts described in this and the next section as one possible source of legal accommodation for our conclusions.

One might also suggest that the problem of fitting trust law to pension trusts is really only a subset of another problem: the task of applying trust law to trusts. Trust law is, in essence, a series of judicially created norms that guide and inform a court's discretion in sorting out problems concerning the relationships and responsibilities of the real people who are parties to trusts. It is hardly a startling insight to suggest that any set of generalizations about human behavior, even when framed as legal rules, can only take us so far in answering hard questions, whether those questions arise in the context of a pension plan or a relatively simple trust to pay for the education of a minor.

Parties to a Trust

There are three parties to a trust: the settlor, the trustee, and the beneficiary. The settlor is the person who creates a trust, the trustee is the person to whom the trust property is transferred, and the beneficiary is the person for whose benefit the trust was created and the property transferred. Nominally, the employer is the settlor of a pension trust,

---

[7] Fischel & Langbein, *ERISA's Fundamental Contradiction: The Exclusive Benefit Rule* (April 18, 1988, draft paper).

the employees are the beneficiaries, and the trustee is the person or institution to which the employer transfers contributions to the pension plan, although we will later examine whether some of the parties to a pension plan play more than one role (e.g., is the employee, who presumably gives up cash wages to participate in a pension plan, really a settlor; is an employer, who hopes the pension plan will breed long employee tenures, a beneficiary?).

The settlor. The settlor of a trust creates the trust. Generally, the settlor contributes property to a trustee of its initial selection, for the benefit of ascertainable beneficiaries. In the case of pension plans, the settlor will generally be the employer, although in negotiated pension plans the union and the employer both may lay claim to the settlor function.

One important and recurring power the settlor has at the time the trust is created is to create a private trust law that governs that particular trust, a private law that might vary fundamental trust principles.[8] Thus, for example, the settlor might create a trust that specifies that the trust property will be invested only in a particular type of property, even though that property might be an improper investment under the common law of trusts.

The settlor also may reserve a power to amend, or terminate, the trust, even though such amendment might be adverse to the interests of the trust beneficiary. In this decade, we have seen the power to terminate a trust exercised by many employers to recover trust property from pension plans.[9]

In the case of a pension plan, the trust may have contractual aspects that bind the settlor to certain courses of action, although many, if not most, carefully drafted pension plans before ERISA expressly disclaimed any contractual obligations on the part of the employer.[10]

The trustee. The settlor will generally select a trustee to whom the trust corpus is transferred. The trustee takes legal ownership to the property and is thereby entrusted with the property's management and ultimate disposition to or for the use of the beneficiary. The trustee can be a natural person or a corporation whose charter lawfully permits it to serve as a trustee.

A settlor may appoint more than one trustee. The general rule is

---

[8] Fratcher, *Scott on Trusts* (4th ed. 1987) § 4.

[9] *See* Ippolito, *Issues Surrounding Pension Terminations for Reversions,* 5 Am. J. Tax P'lcy 81 (1986); Stein, *Raiders of the Corporate Pension Plan: The Reversion of Excess Assets to the Employer,* 5 Am. J. Tax P'lcy 117 (1986).

[10] Harbrecht, *Pension Funds and Economic Power* (1960) 182.

that trust action requires the unanimous agreement of all trustees.[11] The settlor can, however, vary this rule, either by providing that a majority of trustees can authorize trust action, or by dividing specific trust powers among the multiple trustees.[12] The trustees themselves may delegate some of their trust authority to an employee or a cotrustee, but not with respect to significant trust matters, or as George Bogert has written, with respect "to those functions where usual prudent business practice would dictate personal management."[13] A clear example of a nondelegable duty is the duty to invest trust assets. But even here, the trustee could employ others to assist him in selecting proper investments, although the responsibility remains that of the trustee. Again, it should be noted that the settlor can vary trust law and permit expanded delegation.

A trustee who either expressly delegates nondelegable authority to a cotrustee, or through inaction or negligence permits a cotrustee to exercise such authority, will be liable to the trust for any resulting losses. Moreover, a trustee owes a duty to delegate even delegable duties with care and prudence and also may have a duty to monitor the actions of a cotrustee to whom certain authority has been properly delegated.[14]

It should be said that it is not uncommon in pension plans for many aspects of plan administration to be delegated by the plan instrument to a committee, generally selected by the plan sponsor, rather than to the trustee.[15] In such cases, the trustee would act in accordance with the directions of the committee.

Beneficiaries. The settlor determines the beneficiaries of a trust at the time of the trust's creation. A trust may name one or more persons, or a class of persons, as beneficiaries.[16] In the case of pension plans, the beneficiaries are the group of covered employees and their dependents who may become entitled to plan benefits.

Permissibility of dual trust capacities. As a matter of mechanics, a single person could settle a trust naming himself as both the sole trustee and the sole beneficiary. Such a trust, however, would have no substance, and there are cases holding that the legal and beneficial

---

[11] Fratcher, *Scott on Trusts* (4th ed. 1987) § 194. The requirement does not, however, apply to charitable trusts.

[12] Fratcher, *Scott on Trusts* (4th ed. 1987) § 194.

[13] Bogert, *Trusts and Trustees* (4th ed. 1980) § 555.

[14] *Restatement of Trusts Second* § 171(k); Fratcher, *Scott on Trusts* (4th ed. 1987) § 224.3.

[15] *See, e.g.,* Rakness v. Swift & Co., 147 N.W. 2d 567 (Minn. 1966) (pension committee).

[16] Fratcher, *Scott on Trusts* (4th ed. 1987) § 112.

interests in the trust property merge when a single person is the sole trustee and the sole beneficiary.[17] It is, however, permissible for a settlor to name himself either trustee or beneficiary of a trust, although special limitations may apply in such cases, particularly with respect to third parties who deal with either the settlor or the trust.[18] Moreover, there are cases that have permitted a person to be both trustee and beneficiary, so long as there were either multiple trustees or multiple beneficiaries;[19] there are, however, also cases that hold the contrary because of the conflicts of interest that are latent in such cases.[20] It is true, however, that under common law it was permissible for a settlor to appoint trustees with an interest in the trust corpus, a practice that we shall later see ERISA permitted to continue with respect to pension trusts.

The Trustee's Duty of Undivided Loyalty to the Beneficiary

The common law of trusts imposes an unyielding duty on the trustee to administer the trust in the sole interest of the beneficiaries. This duty proscribes self-dealing of any sort on the part of the trustee. The principle, although obviously reaching situations in which the trustee has in fact overreached, applies even in cases that are substantively fair to the trust at the time of the transaction. Thus, the rule is in large measure a prophylactic, designed to prevent all self-dealing.

The broad reach of the duty has been explained as a reflection of "the well-known quality of human nature that it is extremely difficult, or perhaps impossible, for an individual to act fairly in the interests of others whom he represents and at the same time to consider his own financial advantages."[21] It can also be justified as a means of excusing judges, and trust beneficiaries, from the difficult task of assessing a transaction's fairness (in a procedural sense) after the fact.

A transaction between a trustee and a trust is not void, only voidable.[22] In other words, a transaction that violates the duty of loyalty can be ratified by the trust beneficiaries. The ratification, however, has to be unanimous, and any single beneficiary can have a disloyal transaction remedied.[23] (A court in fashioning an appropriate remedy pre-

---

[17] *See, e.g.,* Morsman v. Comm't, 90 F.2d 18 (8th Cir.), *cert. denied,* 302 U.S. 701 (1937); *Restatement of Trusts Second* § 99(5).

[18] *Restatement of Trusts Second* § 100.

[19] *Restatement of Trusts Second* § 99.

[20] Fratcher, *Scott on Trusts* (4th ed. 1987) § 99.3, n.11.

[21] G. Bogert, *Law of Trusts* (1963) 249.

[22] Fratcher, *Scott on Trusts* (4th ed. 1987) § 205, 216.

[23] Fratcher, *Scott on Trusts* (4th ed. 1987) § 216.2.

sumably could take into account the view of the majority of beneficiaries.)

Another interesting question is whether a trust settlor could excuse the trustee from the duty of loyalty. For example, a plan sponsor might establish a pension trust that provides that the trust will enter into purchase, sale, or lease transactions with the trustee, or that the trust will purchase stock of the trustee. Such transactions would violate the duty of loyalty. As already mentioned, however, settlors can create private trust law, and settlors may name themselves trust beneficiaries. However, the settlor cannot totally abrogate the duty of loyalty, for doing so would effectively place the beneficial interest in the hands of the trustee, thus negating the trust relationship.

We have thus far considered the duty of loyalty in the context of self-dealing; the discussion has assumed that a trustee appointed by the employer will be acting on behalf of the employer. In self-dealing cases, the only inquiry the court must make is whether there was self-dealing, a relatively simple inquiry. But the duty of loyalty also extends to another situation: when the trustee acts to benefit a third party rather than the beneficiaries.[24] Here a court faces a more difficult inquiry: whether the trustee's subjective intent was to benefit, or primarily to benefit, the third party.[25]

This distinction between self-dealing and acting for the benefit of third parties has relevance to pension trusts, where employees of the plan sponsor often serve as trustees of the plan.[26] If the trustee is considered a deputy of the employer, any transaction between the plan and plan sponsor presumably would be self-dealing and would be proscribed; however, if the trustee is conceded theoretical independence, transactions between the sponsor and the plan might not violate the duty of loyalty unless the trustee acted for the purpose of benefiting the sponsor. This presents an interesting question for such independent trustees: how much can the trustee consider benefit to the employer? In one celebrated case, *Blankenship* v. *Boyle*,[27] the court held that the trustees violated the duty of loyalty in making certain investments where the trustee's *primary* purpose in making such investments was to benefit the union plan sponsor. *Blankenship* is considered further in the discussion of impartiality, which appears later in this section.[28]

---

[24] Fratcher, *Scott on Trusts* (4th ed. 1987) § 170; *Restatement of Trusts Second* § 170(1), comment (q).

[25] Id.

[26] *See, e.g.*, Foss v. Mahal, 230 N.W. 2d 604 (Minn. 1975) (employee of plan sponsor a trustee).

[27] 329 F.Supp 1089 (D.D.C. 1981).

[28] *See* p. 23, infra.

Duty to Exercise Discretion Reasonably: Proscription against Arbitrary and Capricious Behavior

A trustee performs far too many functions for the settlor to provide explicit instructions that will guide the trustee with perpetual certainty through each trust decision. The idea of the trust is, to a large extent, the settlor's selective transfer to the trustee of some of the settlor's discretion over the trust property. Much of trust law is concerned with identifying what discretion was transferred and how that discretion is exercised properly.

From this perspective, the strict standards of the duty of loyalty may be explained as an instance of the settlor withholding discretion to use the property to benefit the trustee or a third party; the trustee simply has no discretion to act disloyally to the trust beneficiaries. There are, however, significant areas of trust law in which the trustee does have discretion to act; here trust law defines the standards that govern the proper exercise of such discretion. In effect, trust law incorporates the fiduciary standards it presumes the settlor would have specified. Again, it should be borne in mind that the settlor can expand or limit the standards the law would otherwise impose.

There are two particular areas of discretionary trustee conduct: dealings with trust beneficiaries and dealings with trust property. The standards for dealing with trust property are considered in the paper's next section; here, we are concerned with issues of trust administration (i.e., dealings with the beneficiaries, particularly with respect to plan benefits). The *Restatement of Trusts* speaks generally of control of a trustee's discretionary powers, and Professor Scott in his treatise observes that

> courts will not control his exercise [of discretion] as long as he does not exceed the limits of discretion conferred upon him. . . . This ordinarily means that so long as he acts not only in good faith and from proper motives, but also within the bounds of a reasonable judgment, the court will not interfere; but the court will interfere when he acts outside the bounds of a reasonable judgment. In other words, although there is a field, often a wide field, within which the trustee may determine whether to act or not and when and how to act, yet beyond that field the court will control him. How wide that field is depends upon the terms of the trust, the nature of the power, and all circumstances.[29]

---

[29] Fratcher, *Scott on Trusts* (4th ed. 1987) § 187.

Discussion of the control of discretionary powers is often muddled and sometimes confused with the analytically distinct duty of loyalty. As we shall see, the discussion is muddled because the hard questions involve how a trustee should exercise discretion in hard situations; to speak of a generalized duty to exercise discretion reasonably does not sufficiently inform our judgment to make judicial determinations predictable.

The trust standards for control of discretionary fiduciary powers were incorporated into the Labor Management Relations Act (LMRA) by federal courts with respect to union pension trusts. The federal courts, although not without dissenters, came to express these standards as a proscription against arbitrary and capricious conduct: "Trustees, like all fiduciaries, are subject to judicial correction in a proper case upon a showing that they have acted arbitrarily or capriciously towards one of the persons to whom their trust obligations run."[30] The LMRA arbitrary and capricious formulation of the discretionary standard of review has become a fixture in the vocabulary of the pension community.

It is also worth noting that the arbitrary and capricious formula was developed under the rubric of section 301(c)(5) of the LMRA, which generally requires a union pension or welfare fund to be administered "for the sole and exclusive benefit of the employees of such employer, and their families and dependents." The federal courts were able to divine from this language a duty to avoid arbitrary and capricious actions, for such actions would be contrary to the exclusive benefit of the employees.[31] Courts, again not unanimously, used this duty as a basis for jurisdiction under LMRA,[32] which did not explicitly provide for jurisdiction of participant actions for benefits.

In effect, the courts fashioned a standard for judging a trustee's exercise of discretion from a statute whose language seems designed to impose a duty of loyalty. This odd parentage has created some confusion concerning the purpose and function of the arbitrary and capricious standard under the LMRA.

There are four situations in which the proscription against arbitrary

---

[30] Kosty v. Lewis, 319 F.2d 744, 747 (D.C.Cir. 1963), *cert. denied,* 375 U.S. 964 (1964).

[31] Welch & Wilson, *Applicability of Traditional Principles of Trust Law to Union and Management Representatives Administering Taft-Hartley Trusts,* 23 Lab. L. J. 671 (1972); Comment, *The Arbitrary and Capricious Standard Under ERISA: Its Origins and Application,* 23 Duq. L. Rev. 1033, 1037-41 (1985).

[32] *Compare, e.g.,* Insley v. Joyce, 330 F.Supp. 1228 (N.D. Ill. 1971) (finding jurisdiction) *with* Haley v. Palatnik, 378 F.Supp. 499 (S.D.N.Y. 1974) (not finding jurisdiction), *rev'd on other grds.,* 509 F.2d 1038 (2d Cir. 1975).

and capricious conduct might have application, each of which warrant separate consideration.

Trustee action affecting only particular participant or class of participant. In this situation, where the trustee's decision affects only a particular participant or class of participant, the trustee's discretion should be entitled to the greatest degree of deference. An example of such a situation might be the decision whether to permit a retired employee to select a lump sum benefit rather than a life annuity. It presumably would be proper for the trustee to make such a decision on the basis of the perceived ability of the participant to invest and conserve the property to meet expenses during retirement. Even such a decision could, however, be set aside if the trustee's decision that the participant was imprudent was unreasonable or not based on proper factual inquiry, or if the trustee's application of the standard itself was only selectively, that is, arbitrarily, applied.

Trustee decision in which participants (or classes of participants) have competing interests. Some trustee decisions involve allocating limited trust resources among competing classes of beneficiaries. In such cases, the trustee should again be given wide latitude to make a decision based on his best judgment.

Trustee decision involving conflicting interest of plan participant and plan sponsor. A trustee's decision with respect to participant entitlements may involve a participant interest that conflicts directly with that of the plan sponsor. A decision that grants a participant benefits in a defined benefit plan, for example, might result either in an increase in plan funding requirements or in a reduction of plan surplus that might someday revert to the employer.

Trust law raises some interesting questions in this situation, but offers no readily apparent solutions. On one level, the situation seems to implicate the duty of loyalty, since the interest of the plan sponsor is directly adverse to the plan participant. But a defined benefit pension trust certainly contemplates that the trustee will make benefit decisions, and any benefit decision will have some impact, favorable or unfavorable, on the plan sponsor.

Once we concede that the trustee is in a position to make a benefit decision, there are two possible approaches. One is the approach that had been used in many LMRA cases: that the trustee's benefit decision can only be challenged in court as being arbitrary and capricious. Under such an approach, what would be forbidden to the trustee in a benefit entitlement case would be to act for the benefit of the plan sponsor rather than for the benefit of the trust participants.[33] In this

---

[33] The trustee would also, of course, be forbidden from varieties of arbitrary conduct other than acting for the self-interest of the plan sponsor.

regard, comments to the *Restatement on Trusts* indicate that a trustee abuses his discretion if he acted from an improper purpose.[34]

This approach, however, presents practical problems, because the subjectivity of the question of motivation ensures that in many cases the question can never be answered with confidence. Moreover, how can we ever trust the bona fides of a decision adverse to a participant if the adverse decision directly benefits the plan sponsor and offers no compensating benefits to the trust fund or any of the fund's beneficiaries? I would suggest that in a world that takes account of reality we would rarely be able to conclude that the plan decision maker has not acted from improper motive.

The second approach is to apply the arbitrary and capricious standard only if we conclude from the trust instrument that the settlor intended benefit decisions to be discretionary rather than ministerial.[35] If we frame our inquiry in these terms, we would need to determine whether the settlor granted discretionary power to the trustee to make benefit determinations. Where a pension plan document defines benefit entitlements that arise in a workplace, we might take the position that the trustee has no discretion but rather must interpret the language in accordance with its legal meaning; that is, to treat the language as contractual. In other words, the trustee's duty with respect to benefit entitlements is to determine whether a court would find a contractual entitlement. Such an approach avoids the troubling issue of granting a trustee discretion to make a decision in which its interests are directly inimical to those of the trust's beneficiaries. Most of trust law is designed to keep trustees from being in a position to make such decisions.

There are some pre-ERISA cases, some arising under the LMRA and some arising under state law, that in fact treat matters relating to benefit entitlements as contractual issues.[36] There are also cases under state common law that used the arbitrary and capricious standard to test benefit decisions, but without exception these cases involve plans that explicitly provided that trustee decisions would be final and binding on participants.[37] Such cases, then, did not turn on trust law per se, but on discretion expressly conferred on the trustee (or an administrative committee that would direct the trustee) by the settlor. In fact, even many of these cases analyze the validity of the benefit determination

---

[34] *Restatement of Trusts Second* § 187, comment e.

[35] *See generally* Fratcher, *Scott on Trusts* (4th ed. 1987) § 171.

[36] Hurd v. Illinois Bell Telephone Co., 136 F.Supp. 125 (N.D.Ill. 1955), *affirmed,* 234 F.2d 942 (7th Cir. 1956); Hobbs v. Lewis, 159 F.Supp. 282 (D.D.C. 1958).

[37] *See, e.g.,* Menke v. Thompson, 140 F.2d 786 (8th Cir. 1944); Judge. v. Kortenhaus, 192 A.2d 320 (1963).

with respect to contractual rather than trust principles; in such cases, the court treats the pension plan as a contract in which the contract provides that disputed matters will be determined by the employer.[38]

I would thus conclude that unless the pension plan expressly committed benefit decisions to trustee discretion, trust law would assume that benefit entitlement is a contractual question; the trustee performs only a ministerial function, albeit a difficult one: predicting how a court would decide a contractual issue. It is interesting to note that at least one federal circuit court applying Minnesota law held that a private pension plan was a contract of adhesion, to be construed against the employer.[39]

Trustee decision affecting both plan sponsor and competing classes of participants. There are situations in which the plan sponsor has an interest that is aligned with one of two competing classes of beneficiaries. For example, in some pension plans the trustee's responsibilities may include amending the plan to improve benefits; the employer, for general corporate reasons, may wish the trustee to create a subsidized early retirement benefit that is limited to a window period, which would favor certain employees over other plan participants. Or a trustee may have to decide whether to pay separating employees either a lump sum or deferred benefit from a profit-sharing plan. A trust policy against paying such benefits to key employees, who may have a strong hand in producing profits and thus increasing employer contributions to the plan, would benefit most plan participants by keeping a handcuff on key employees (to the extent the nonavailability of a lump sum benefit is a disincentive to quitting); it would also benefit the employer who wishes to retain the employee. Pre-ERISA law apparently gave the trustee latitude in decision-making authority in these situations.[40]

An interesting point can be made about the pure conflict situations discussed above. It is possible to argue that when a trustee makes a decision that causes an employer to increase contributions to a plan, the trustee is increasing the probability that the employer will decide to make up its losses by amending the plan to reduce future benefits for other beneficiaries, by terminating the plan, or by refusing to increase future plan contributions, thereby forcing the trustee to allocate scarce

---

[38] Gitelson v. Du Pont, 215 N.E.2d (N.Y.Ct.App. 1966) ("The rights of the plaintiff under the plan are contract rights [but] are limited by the provisions of the contract.")

[39] Landro v. Glendenning Motorways, Inc. 625 F.2d 1344 (1980); *see also* Foss v. Mahal, 230 N.W.2d 604 (Minn. 1975) (refusing to accord deference to trustee decision as to benefit eligibility since not a matter of trust administration).

[40] *See, e.g.,* Lano v. Rochester Germicide Co., 113 N.W.2d 460 (Minn. 1962).

trust resources among too many deserving claimants. Viewed from this perspective, there may be many decisions that seem only to pit employer against participant where in fact the employer's interest (i.e., keeping contributions at an acceptable level) is aligned with the interest of other participants, who stand to lose if the employer can strap them with the unanticipated costs. Accepting this perspective, however, is something else again, for we can only do so if we accept the premise that the employer can recoup lost costs from other plan participants. Whether this premise can be accepted in a given situation may hinge on our understanding of how a given market for labor functions.

Duties with Respect to Trust Property

Trust law includes an imposing amalgam of rule, license, and standard for a trustee's relationship with trust property. The two most general, and most important, such rules are commonly referred to as the prudent man rule and the duty to diversify. In this section we will consider these two rules and also how they affect trustee authority to base investment decisions on social and moral considerations.

In some respects these rules may be considered merely a subset of the proposition that a trustee can only exercise discretion reasonably. The settlor transfers property to the trustee and thereby accords the trustee discretion to manage the property. The law assumes that the settlor would wish the discretion exercised for the purpose of the trust, which generally is to benefit the trust beneficiaries through maximizing return with due emphasis placed on the safety of investment. Hence the prudent man rule and the duty to diversify.

Prudent man rule. Trust law has long imposed a duty of prudence on trustees. The *Restatement of Trusts* has stated the standard as that of a person of ordinary prudence in dealing with his own property.[41] The standard requires the trustee to display ordinary prudence, even though the trustee might lack ordinary skill or might be less risk averse than a person of ordinary prudence. A trustee whose skill is greater than ordinary, however, may have liability even though his actions would have been appropriate for a person of ordinary prudence, especially if the trustee was selected because of his greater skill. This principle often will apply to institutional trustees, such as banks.

To say that the standard requires a trustee to exhibit the skill and care of a person of ordinary prudence does not say enough, for we must next ask: the skill and care of a person of ordinary prudence doing

---

[41] *Restatement of Trusts Second* §§ 174, 227.

what? The *Restatement of Trusts* has supplied an answer here as well: obtaining a reasonable rate of return while giving due regard to the conservation of the trust property. The rule was first articulated in *Harvard College* v. *Amory*,[42] a landmark case in which Harvard University argued that a trustee acted improperly by investing in the stock of manufacturing and insurance companies. The rule was expressed with the following language:

> [The trustee] shall conduct himself faithfully and exercise a sound discretion. He is to observe how men of prudence, discretion and intelligence manage their own affairs, not in regard to speculation, but in regard to the permanent disposition of their funds, considering the probable income, as well the probable safety of the capital to be invested.

The standard is sufficiently vague to permit trustees' wide latitude in permissible investments; it is also sufficiently vague to permit dissatisfied beneficiaries to second guess decisions that turned out badly. Courts, however, have tolerated decisions that in retrospect look bad, so long as they were supportable at the time of the investment.[43] Thus, a trustee in making an investment generally would want to demonstrate that his actions were taken only after careful investigation and deliberation about each choice of investment.

There are some investments, however, that a trustee may not make under the common-law prudent man rule, especially investments of a speculative nature. For example, trustees are not permitted to purchase securities on margin or to invest in speculative securities or the securities of new industries.[44] It is also generally true that a trustee cannot use trust funds to carry on a business or to invest in property for the sole purpose of resale. In addition, most states have their own particular lists of proper investments that may impose additional limitations on the trustee, but the modern trend has been toward fewer restrictions.[45] Moreover, the settlor in establishing the trust generally may permit investments that would otherwise be improper under state law or may prohibit investments that would otherwise be proper.

Trust law generally tests the rule of prudence on an investment-by-investment basis (rather than on a portfolio-wide basis), which can have the unfortunate effect of permitting beneficiaries to attack soured

---

[42] 9 Pick. 446 (Mass. 1830).

[43] *E.g.*, Matter of Clark, 257 N.Y. 132 (1931).

[44] Fratcher, *Scott on Trusts* (4th ed. 1987) § 227.4.

[45] Fratcher, *Scott on Trusts* (4th ed. 1987) 227.5. Historically, many states prohibited investments in common stock, and some states retain this restriction. Id.

investments even though the overall performance of the trust has been strong.[46] However, the *Restatement of Trusts* states that in deciding on whether an investment is reasonable, the factors a trustee should consider include market conditions, the nature of other trust investments, and the particular needs of the trust, all of which might help a trustee to defend particular investments.[47]

Duty to diversify. Trust law generally imposes a duty on the trustee to diversify investments. The purpose of this duty is to reduce the risk of large loss to the trust estate by ensuring a portfolio sufficiently diverse as to minimize loss resulting from hazards common to similar investments. Although the duty is often considered a responsibility separate and distinct from the general prudence requirement, it may also be understood as an application of the prudent man rule, since a prudent person would select every investment with at least some eye to whether the particular investment added to or subtracted from the portfolio's diversity. It merits note that through the diversity rule an otherwise prudent investment might have been rendered imprudent, but that portfolio concerns could not make an otherwise imprudent investment acceptable.

There are relatively few cases, or statutes, that provide specific standards to gauge whether a trustee has satisfied a diversification requirement. However, trustees may violate the duty where trust assets are too heavily invested in a single company,[48] in a single industry,[49] in a single variety of security,[50] or a single geographic region.[51] Courts have indicated tolerance for investments as large as 22 percent of a trust fund of a railroad company,[52] but an English court found that an investment of as little as 10 percent in a single bank was too high.[53] Undoubtedly, much depends on circumstances. For example, a small trust fund has less ability to diversify than a large one, and some investments,

---

[46] If a gain and loss result from a single branch of trust, courts may permit the gain to offset the loss for purposes of computing the loss for which the trustee must account. *See* Fratcher, *Scott on Trusts* 2d § 213. There can, however, be issues concerning whether certain acts constitute only a single breach of trust.

[47] *Restatement of Trusts Second* 227, comment o.

[48] Dickson, Appellant, 152 Mass. 184 (1890) (cited in Fratcher, *Scott on Trusts* (4th ed. 1987) § 228).

[49] In re Ward, 121 N.J.Eq. 555 (1936).

[50] Wis. Stat. § 320.02.

[51] Penn. Co. for Insurance on Lives & Granting Annuities v. Gilmore, 142 N.J.Eq. 27 (1948) (cited in Fratcher, *Scott on Trusts* (4th ed. 1987) § 228).

[52] Dickinson, Appellant, 25 N.E. 99 (Mass. 1890) (cited in Fratcher, *Scott on Trusts* (4th ed. 1987) § 228).

[53] Astbury v. Beastley, 17 W.R. 638 (1869) (cited in Fratcher, *Scott on Trusts* (4th ed. 1987) § 228).

such as Treasury bills and highly rated corporate bonds, are safer than others.

Social investing. The prudent person of trust law invests with a mind to maximize return while minimizing loss; the person of ordinary prudence under the trust law standard does not take into account factors that are irrelevant to, or even in conflict with, maximizing return. Trustees of pension plans, however, sometimes might consider factors in selecting investments that conflict with return maximization. When the trustee finds these factors compelling, he engages in what has been called *social investing*.

There are two types of social investing, which I will call *moral* social investing and *pecuniary* social investing. Moral social investing occurs when a trustee limits investments to firms or projects providing a perceived broadly focused social good (e.g., refusing to invest in firms that break unions or do business in South Africa). The oxymoronic pecuniary social investing refers to when a trustee considers a lower return in exchange for other pecuniary benefits for at least some of the plan participants (e.g., an investment in bonds of the employer in order to preserve the jobs of plan participants). The issues raised by pecuniary social investing are distinct from those of moral social investing, and one could argue that pecuniary social investing is not social investing at all. But commentary has often considered the two in tandem, and I will conform to this approach, although attempting to give each its separate due.

Social investing raises two difficult questions. The first is whether trust law permits social investing in the absence of express license from the settlor. The second question assumes a negative answer to the first and asks whether settlor authorization or plan participant ratification may permit what otherwise would not be tolerated.

There are at least three justifications for permitting social investing under trust law, one of which is relevant to all social investing, one to moral social investing only, and one to pecuniary social investing only.

Social investments do not necessarily violate trust prudence and diversification standards. Social investing may be permitted so long as the investments will produce a rate of return equivalent to other investments, since if the rate of return is equivalent to other investments, the prudent man rule will be satisfied.

Judge Posner and Professor Langbein have argued that because finance theory has demonstrated that returns are maximized through investment in broad-based market funds, such as the S&P 500, which combine optimal levels of diversification with minimal management charges, use of other investment strategies may violate the trustee's duty of diversification.[54] Excluding stock from inclusion in a trust portfolio on social grounds is inimical to this approach to investing and accordingly may violate the trustee's duty to diversify. However, there does not appear as yet to be any case that expressly adopts this theory of diversification; it would be difficult at present to conclude that social investing necessarily violates judicial understanding of the duty to diversify for this reason.

Part of Posner and Langbein's argument, however, is that social investing subjects the trust to extra transaction costs. These costs will always reduce a plan's net rate of return and should reduce our confidence that a plan with a social investment program will ordinarily be able to obtain a rate of return equivalent to that which could otherwise be realized.

Moral social investing is permissible because of its societal benefit. Professor Scott, in his treatise on trusts, has argued that a trustee "is entitled to consider the welfare of the community, and refrain from allowing the use of the funds in a manner detrimental to society,"[55] even though returns are thereby decreased. Thus, a trustee may properly consider "such matters as pollution, race discrimination, fair employment, and consumer responsibility."[56] Posner and Langbein criticize this view as inconsistent with both the rule of prudence and the duty to diversify. There are, so far as I know, no cases accepting Professor Scott's view, although in the corporate law area there has been an emergent view tolerant of directorial consideration of factors other than direct benefit to the shareholders.[57] I should also note that some have argued that moral concerns often track financial concerns: Investments in South Africa, for example, might subject companies to high levels of risk because of the disruptions caused by the morally repugnant behavior of Pretoria. If this were true, however, avoidance of the investment would not have been due to social considerations but financial ones and thus would be removed from the concerns applicable to social investing. In addition, as Professor Langbein and Judge Posner have noted, this view ignores the fact that the market should adjust equity prices to account for the risks posed by doing business in South Africa:

---

[54] Langbein & Posner, *Social Investing and the Law of Trusts,* 79 Mich. L. Rev. 72 (1980).

[55] Fratcher, *Scott on Trusts* (4th ed. 1987) § 227.17.

[56] Id.

[57] American Law Institute, *Principles of Corporate Governance* (Tent. Draft No. 2 1984) 2.01 (noting that corporation may devote resources to public welfare, humanitarian, educational, and philanthropic purposes). *But see* Fischel, *The Corporate Governance Movement,* 35 Vand. L. Rev. 1259, 1273 (1982) (arguing that consideration of moral or social obligations by corporation is "a fundamental error").

The true loss to the plan may come trom extra transaction costs and the loss of fund diversity by limiting investments to "socially acceptable ones."

Pecuniary social investing is permissible because it benefits plan participants. It is arguable that in determining a prudent investment the trustee should be permitted to look beyond rate of return on investment to whether an investment will otherwise benefit plan participants. For example, a trustee might wish to invest in a hospital in a company town that lacks adequate medical resources, for such a hospital will benefit participants. Or a trustee may wish to lend money to the plan sponsor to ensure the fiscal health of the sponsor and thus preserve the jobs of participants. Should the trustee be precluded from making such investments if they will generate lower rates of return than other available investments with comparable levels of risk or if they will subject the trust to undue risk because of a lack of diversity?

In *Cowan* v. *Scargill*, a British Chancery decision, the court suggested a negative answer to these questions.[58] The case presented the question whether union trustees for a mine workers' pension trust could oppose certain investments that might harm the British mining industry and the union. The court indicated that although there are times when social investing might be proper because of a virtual unanimity of view on the part of the trust beneficiaries, that could not be the case in a pension trust that covered many people for whom the welfare of the union and mining industry would not have been issues meriting sacrifice of return. Moreover, the court also observed that "under a trust for the provision of financial benefits the burden would rest, and rest heavy, on him who asserts that it is for the benefit of the beneficiaries as a whole to receive less by reason of the exclusion of the possibly more profitable forms of investments."

A contrary view—that trustees should be able to take into account benefits that may reduce financial returns—is easiest to justify when the benefit to plan participants will also contribute to the health of the pension fund; for example, in *Withers* v. *Teacher's Retirement System of the City of New York*,[59] the trust invested in bonds of New York City, notwithstanding lower returns given the level of risk. The investments, by forestalling the city's insolvency, made layoffs of teachers less probable. When these investments were challenged, however, the court discounted the possible preservation of jobs as a trustee motive, but stated

[58] 3 W.L.R. 501 (Ch.Div. 1984). The case discusses two American decisions on social investing, Blankenship v. Boyle and Withers v. Teacher's Retirement System of the City of New York, each of which is discussed below.

[59] 447 F.Supp. 1248 (S.D.N.Y. 1978).

that it would approve the trustees' actions because the investments increased the probability that the city would avoid bankruptcy and thus be able to meet its contributory obligations to the trust. Even if we accept the court's characterization of the trustee motive, we face something very much like the pecuniary social investing issue: should the trustees consider what is best for the future of the pension plan on any basis but maximizing return? Here the court, in effect, considered the value of future plan contributions.

This type of question may arise elsewhere, for example in a hostile takeover situation if the trustees believe the acquiror will close a plant whose employees are plan participants or will terminate the pension fund to recover residual assets. If the trustee is positioned with economic power sufficient to affect the takeover, should it be permitted to use the power to attempt to prevent it?

The observation in the *Cowan* decision on the rationale for pecuniary social investing may warrant restatement in closing this discussion: Most pecuniary social investing will benefit only some participants while all participants will suffer the reduced return.[60] One might respond, however, that trustees often face decisions involving the allocation of trust resources in a way that will benefit some beneficiaries at a cost to others.

The second set of issues involves the ability of either the settlor, or the beneficiary, to permit social investing in the face of any legal prohibitions against it. I have already indicated that the law is in an unsettled period regarding the propriety of social investing, but for purposes of this discussion I will assume that trust principles would generally prohibit it.

As we have already seen, ordinarily the settlor does enjoy the right to expand a trustee's powers through language in the trust document including the power to engage in social investing; similarly, beneficiaries, acting in unanimity, may ratify a trustee's actions. In a pension plan of any size, however, it is improbable that the plan participants will ever be of one mind on social investing, making ratification improbable.

There are three (perhaps four) types of pension situations in which ratification or authorization might arise: defined benefit plan in which the employer has promised to fund a particular level of benefits, defined benefit plans in which the level of benefits is determined by the

---

[60] For instance, Professors Langbein and Fischel, in *ERISA's Fundamental Contradiction: The Exclusive Benefit Rule,* point to *Withers* as an example of a case where trustee action protected the jobs of union members, but hurt all beneficiaries under the trust, including those who had already retired.

size of the trust fund, and defined contribution plans (in which employees might or might not be given authority to direct investments for their own account).

There does not appear to be any reason why the settlor could not as part of the trust instrument direct that investments be made on some basis other than maximization of return; however, in a case where authorization of such investments is effected through amendment of the trust document in an established plan, the beneficiaries in either the second category of defined benefit plan or a defined contribution plan would suffer a capital loss if such amendment applied not only to future contributions by the settlor but also to the trust accumulation at the time of the amendment. Assuming that the settlor has reserved the power to amend the trust, there would not seem to be any clear trust principle to prevent such an amendment, even though it harms the trust participants. The participants, if they are to challenge such an amendment, would presumably have to rely on contractual principles to redress any harm caused them.

Ratification by beneficiaries presents the reverse side of the looking glass: Ratification in the first category of defined benefit plan may saddle the employer with losses, since the employer will have to increase contributions. As a practical matter, however, it is improbable that the beneficiaries will be able to pressure the trustee in this category of plan to engage in social investing, first because the trustee will only be insulated from liability if the social investing is ratified by *all* participants, and second, because the trustee's loyalty generally will run to the settlor, who in all probability selected him and reserved the right to replace him.

Posner and Langbein have argued that the case for social investing is easiest in participant-directed defined contribution plans, since the only party affected by the social investing is the individual participant who authorized it. The Posner/Langbein position seems unassailable under trust common law.

Duty to Vote Shares

Trust law imposes a duty on trustees to vote shares of stock in the interest of the beneficiaries. The standard by which trustee action is judged is whether he abused his discretion;[61] however, the duty of loyalty might become applicable where the trustee had a personal stake in the outcome of a vote (for example, in a fight to depose current

[61] Fratcher, *Scott on Trusts* (4th ed. 1987) § 193.1.

management, where the trustee is part of such management or is an officer of a corporate fiduciary which has ties to current management). The settlor, however, can alter these rules by providing that the trustee shall vote in a particular manner, including conforming to directions of either the settlor or beneficiary.

Voting of shares can raise issues parallel to those raised by social investing: When may the trustee's vote be based, at least in part, on considerations other than maximizing return while minimizing risk? Posner and Langbein have argued that social share voting is more difficult to justify than social investing, since social voting, if successful, might impose actual capital loss on the plan.[62]

Duty of Impartiality

In multibeneficiary trusts, the trustee is subject to a duty of impartiality when making decisions whose impact would not be uniform among all beneficiaries.[63] The possibility of such conflicts in a pension trust is manifold, arising in decisions of trust administration and trust investment. For example, a trust with insufficient resources to satisfy all benefit promises may have to decide which promises to fulfill; a trustee may have to decide whether to make a risky investment in an employer, which will preserve the jobs of active employees but threaten the security of the matured benefit promises to retirees. We have already seen this above.

In making these decisions, the trustee may receive some direction from the trust instrument, but more probably will be forced to make a decision without any express guidance. The duty of impartiality itself offers only minimal guidance, for there are often conflicts in which the competing interests of beneficiaries cannot be brought into perfect stasis, and thus such conflict must be resolved in a manner that will favor some beneficiaries over others. To say the trustee must act impartially in such a situation is to say only that a trustee must make a fair choice without indicating how fairness should be determined by the trustee or judged by a court. Thus, in judging decisions that putatively raise issues of impartiality, necessity may push courts into assessing (at least *sub rosa*) whether the trustee has violated some other duty.

There are three duties that might be violated in a situation raising impartiality concerns: the duty to avoid arbitrary and capricious action, the duty of prudence, and the duty of loyalty (which might arise if the

---

[62] Langbein and Posner, *Social Investing and the Law of Trusts,* 79 Mich. L. Rev. 72, 73–74, n.8 (1980).

[63] *Restatement of Trusts Second* § 183.

decision will have an impact on the plan sponsor). Because these duties impose different standards of fiduciary conduct, a court's choice of which duty may have been violated will in large measure determine whether a trustee is at fault.

Generally, the court will be faced with one of two sets of possible standards: in cases of trust administration, either the duty to avoid arbitrary and capricious action or the duty of loyalty; and in cases involving investments, either the duty of prudence or the duty of loyalty. The case of *Blankenship* v. *Boyle*,[64] a pre-ERISA case, illustrates how a court dealt with each type of impartiality problem by selecting the duty appropriate to the particular problem.

Mr. Blankenship was a member of the United Mine Workers of America (UMWA) and a participant in its Health and Retirement Funds. Mr. Blankenship brought a class action that alleged various fiduciary breaches by fund trustees. The trust was a Taft-Hartley trust and was managed by a union, management, and neutral trustee. There are two particular alleged breaches that I want to focus on, each of which raises conceivable issues of impartiality that the district court resolved by applying the strict standards of the duty of loyalty.

The first alleged breach was the trustees' decision to invest in electric utility stock for the purpose of using such stock ownership to pressure the utilities to purchase union coal. This plan, if successful, would have had two salutory effects on younger employees: It would have expanded employment for union miners and in so doing would have increased contributions to the fund (since contributions to the fund were royalties based on union coal tonnage). Professors Langbein and Fischel have suggested that the plan would also have a cost in the probable devaluation of the stock if the utilities had to pay more for union coal. This potential cost was borne by all plan participants, including those who were already retired or were close to retirement, even though these plan participants would not share in the benefits. In fact, the stock's value did decline, although it is not clear that this was attributable to the utility's purchase of union coal.

Professors Langbein and Fischel have taken the position that the trustees' action should have raised a question involving impartiality: whether to make a decision that carried risk for all participants but benefits for only some. The court, however, analyzed the issue as one of loyalty. Since the trustees' primary motive was to benefit the union and

---

[64] 329 F.Supp. 1089 (D.D.C. 1971). I am indebted in this section, especially with respect to discussion of the UMWA Funds' investments in utility stock, to the important insights of Professors Fischel and Langbein in *ERISA's Fundamental Contradiction*, supra note 7.

union coal operators, the action violated the duty of loyalty, even though some incidental benefit might have accrued to the fund. If the issue had been framed as whether the investment had been prudent, the trustees may have prevailed, since the investment in the utility stock was not in itself improper (although Professors Langbein and Fischel suggest that the investment might have been imprudent because the trustees' plan to force purchase of union stock would not only have reduced the value of the stock held by the plan, but also would have been doomed to probable failure since it could have been challenged by other shareholders under the corporate loyalty doctrine).[65] In short, liability resulted because the court decided that the question raised a loyalty issue rather than an issue of prudence.

The second issue involved not an investment decision, but a decision of trust administration. Plan benefits were set by the trustees. On the day the UMWA selected Tony Boyle as president, Boyle caused the plan trustees to increase retirement benefits from $115 to $150. This decision, which took limited funds and directed them to a particular benefit, should have raised an issue of whether the trustees were favoring one class of beneficiaries over another (for example, those who would have preferred increased medical benefits), that is, an issue of impartiality. There were, however, indications that the UMWA leadership raised retirement benefits because of the goodwill such action would engender in the UMWA membership, without any inquiry into whether the fund assets were sufficient to pay such increases. Viewed from the perspective of whether the trustees were within the bounds of their discretion in using limited resources to increase benefits, the decision may well have been substantively defensible, and indeed, the court suggested that it would have been. However, the court held that the union trustee violated his duty of loyalty. (The management and neutral trustee were found to have violated their duties to the plan by allowing themselves to be manipulated by the union trustee, with no independent investigation.)

I should add a final point about both *Blankenship* issues that I suggested might have been resolved differently had they been analyzed as questions of either trustee discretion or trustee prudence. The trustee actions would only have been defensible under these latter standards had a court considered the actions' substance and not the deliberative

---

[65] Professors Langbein and Fischel argue that the court should have viewed the issue as one of impartiality; from this perspective, the authors suggest that the court exaggerated the conflict that existed, since most beneficiaries were also union members. However, Langbein and Fischel believe that the investment was, in any event, imprudent for the reasons suggested in the text.

process undertaken by the trustees. To the extent process is important, the court's finding that the trustees acted with a primary purpose of benefiting the UMWA might well have been sufficient to find against the defendants, even though the decisions themselves could be defended as a reasonable balancing of competing beneficiary interests. As I have already indicated, considering improper purposes—or at least making them controlling factors in a decision—in itself can violate the duty to avoid arbitrary and capricious action and also the duty of prudence. Thus, the result in *Blankenship* may also be explained as the trustees' failure to exercise their discretion properly.

Blankenship presented a case with facts that might have made it relatively easy for a court to infer an improper primary purpose; in most cases we can expect that the primary motivation will not be so easy to pin down. And if the primary motivation is not easy to pin down, a trustee contemplating action that will benefit both the fund and the plan sponsor will have little to help him predict how a court will judge the propriety of his action until after the fact.

Trustee Compensation

Trustees are entitled to compensation for their services in the United States, but individual states have different rules on the determination of compensation.[66] In some states, the compensation will be based on percentages of both the trust corpus and the trust income; in other states, these percentages delineate the upper boundaries of compensation, with a court making a determination about the reasonable value of services rendered. In other states, courts will fix compensation on the basis of the extent of the trustee's stewardship, the skill in which the stewardship was rendered, its degree of success, etc. Of course, the settlor in drafting the trust document may set the trustee's compensation.

A trustee is also entitled to be indemnified for its proper expenses.[67]

Duty to Furnish Information to Beneficiaries

The beneficiaries of a trust are generally entitled to access to information concerning the administration of the trust.[68] The information to

---

[66] Fratcher, *Scott on Trusts* (4th ed. 1987) § 242.

[67] Id. at § 244.

[68] Id. at § 173.

which a beneficiary is entitled includes an inventory of trust property, certain opinions of counsel, vouchers, contracts, etc. The right to information is a separate right with respect to each beneficiary.

Duty to Account to Beneficiaries

The trustee is under a duty to keep accounts indicating all trust receipts and expenditures, including investments, gains, and losses.[69] The trustee is also under a duty to account to the beneficiaries, sometimes on a periodic basis, but also in response to a demand from a beneficiary. A settlor may excuse a trustee from a duty to account, but at least in simple trust and estate cases, courts have been reluctant to give substance to such trust clauses.

Remedies for Breaches by Trustees

Trust law developed in the Court of Chancery and a beneficiary's usual remedy would be an equitable proceeding. The most common equitable remedies that would be sought by beneficiaries against a trustee include the following:

1. Injunction.
   A beneficiary may enjoin a trustee's probable future breach of trust.[70]
2. Specific performance.
   A beneficiary may sue to compel a trustee to enforce the terms of a trust.[71]
3. Redress.
   If a trustee has committed a breach of trust, a beneficiary may bring an action to remedy the breach. The court has considerable flexibility in fashioning an appropriate remedy. Common forms of remedy include requiring the trustee to pay money to the trust and undoing a transaction (for example, the sale of property from the trust to the trustee).[72] The remedy may compensate the trust for actual loss, and may also in some cases cause the trustee to pay the trust the profits he earned through a violation of the requirements of loyalty.

---

[69] Id. at § 172.
[70] Id. at § 199.2.
[71] Id. at § 199.1.
[72] Id. at § 199.3.

4. Removal and Receivership.
   A court may remove a trustee, or appoint a temporary receiver for the trust property, if that is necessary to protect the interests of the beneficiary.[73]

Beneficiaries might also have legal remedies available to them, although these have historically been limited.[74] However, one legal remedy may have relevance to pension plans: an action for damages when a trustee wrongfully withholds trust property that he is under an unconditional duty to pay to a beneficiary.[75] Whether a beneficiary can bring a legal action (when benefits are not paid to him) is of more than academic interest, because the right to a jury trial—denied in equitable proceedings—may hang in the balance.

Spendthrift Trusts

Beneficial interests in trust property are ordinarily subject to sale or other assignment by, and may be reached by creditors of, the beneficiary.[76] A settlor, however, may decide that a beneficiary requires protection from his own imprudence and thus place a clause in the trust restricting free alienability of the beneficial interest. Such clauses, by design, will defeat just claims against the beneficiary, although even here a creditor can reach trust distributions once they are in the beneficiary's hands.

Spendthrift clauses are upheld in many jurisdictions.[77] However, no jurisdiction will sanction a spendthrift clause for a trust in which the settlor is also the beneficiary. Moreover, a spendthrift clause generally would not shield the assets of the trust against a former spouse suing for alimony or child support. Spendthrift clauses were common in pension plans and generally enforced, sometimes because state or federal statutes expressly provided that the interests of beneficiaries in certain pension funds could not be reached by creditors.

Related to the spendthrift trust are the support and discretionary trusts. In such trusts, the beneficiary is entitled only to amounts that the

---

[73] Id. at § 199.4.

[74] Id. at § 198.

[75] Id. at §198.1. The duty to pay the money must be immediate and unconditional; if a beneficiary has a dispute concerning the meaning of the trustee's interpretation of the pension language there may be a question as to whether the obligation to pay the money is in fact unconditional.

[76] Fratcher, *Scott on Trusts* (4th ed. 1987) §§ 132, 147.

[77] *See generally* Fratcher, *Scott on Trusts* (4th ed. 1987) § 151, 152; *see also* E. Griswold, *Spendthrift Trusts* (1936).

trustee determines is proper, subject to reversal only if there is an abuse of discretion. Such trusts also may include an express restriction on alienation. Pension trusts often charge the trustee with responsibility for determining how and when benefits are to be paid (in a lump sum, in installments), and this discretion may frustrate attempts by creditors to reach a participant's interest in the trust, even if the trust does not include a spendthrift clause.

ERISA'S MODIFICATION OF TRUST PRINCIPLES

Congress enacted ERISA in 1974, which put in place a comprehensive federal regulatory scheme for pension and other employee benefit plans. Although ERISA had no clear centerpiece, arguably its most significant feature was its formulation of federal fiduciary principles broadly applicable to almost all employee plans. These fiduciary principles were, to a large extent, borrowed from trust law; the report accompanying the Senate Labor Committee's bill stated that "[t]he fiduciary responsibility section, in essence, codifies and makes applicable to these fiduciaries [of pension plans] certain principles developed in the evolution of the law of trusts."[78]

Congress identified four reasons for thus federalizing trust law. First, Congress believed a uniform national standard should supersede the separate laws of the states. Second, Congress wished to make trust standards applicable to administrators of employee benefit plans that did not employ a trust. Third, Congress wanted to provide plan participants with effective means of remedying fiduciary violations, which meant providing access to the federal courts and requiring more thorough disclosure. Fourth, Congress recognized that traditional trust law had developed through judicial consideration of traditional trust arrangements, generally intrafamily trusts, and that trust principles so developed might not always conform well to the realities and concerns of pension plans.[79] This last purpose is the most significant in providing guidance to the meaning of the standards ERISA defined for the conduct of fiduciaries.

Before beginning our consideration of the particular ERISA fiduciary rules, it may be helpful to identify a theme that runs through ERISA's incorporation of trust concepts: ERISA's provisions are mandatory. In trust law, remember, the settlor can modify trust duties as

---

[78] S. Rep. 93–127, 93d Cong., 1st Sess. (1973) 29.

[79] *See, e.g.,* House Education and Labor Comm. Report on Employee Benefit Security Act of 1973, H. Rep. No.93-533 (1973), at 11–12.

fundamental as the duty of loyalty or the prudent investor rules. This, however, was perhaps what Congress regarded as the aspect of trust law most inappropriate to pension plans, since fiduciary standards are often what stands between an empty and fulfilled pension promise. Thus, ERISA prohibits a settlor from modifying the fiduciary standards Congress created.

A final initial point is that Congress viewed ERISA's written fiduciary standards as a starting line; Congress's incorporation of "certain principles developed in the law of trusts," coupled with its exhortation that pension plans are "quite different from the [private] trust both in purpose and nature," indicates that Congress expected decision makers—the Department of Labor and the courts—to create a federal common law for regulation of pension fiduciary conduct based on the special characteristics of pension plans. In the words of Senator Javits, "It is also intended that a body of federal substantive law will be developed by the courts to deal with issues involving rights and obligations under private welfare and pension plans."

Requirement of Trust and the Expansion of the Concept of Fiduciary

ERISA, with certain exceptions noted below, requires that an employee benefit plan's assets be held in trust and managed and controlled by a trustee.[80] The trust requirement is not applicable to plans that use an insurance contract as a funding vehicle;[81] neither is it applicable to certain custodial account arrangements.[82] This nonapplicability is largely illusory, however, since ERISA subjects the administrators of nontrust funding vehicles to the same fiduciary standards as a trustee.

ERISA, in fact, extends the reach of its trustlike standards beyond that of trustee to all plan fiduciaries, a term that is defined in the act. A person (or entity) is a fiduciary under ERISA to the extent he exercises discretionary authority or discretionary control respecting management or disposition of its assets, renders investment advice for a fee, or has discretionary authority or discretionary responsibility in the administration of the plan.[83] The language of the definition is broadly encompassing. Case law has interpreted the definition of fiduciary liberally; for example, a member of a corporation's board

---

[80] ERISA § 403(a).

[81] ERISA § 403(b)(1), (2).

[82] ERISA § 403(b)(5).

[83] ERISA § 3(21)(A).

of directors is a fiduciary if he has responsibility to name the plan's trustee.[84]

ERISA also requires the plan document to identify one or more fiduciaries as having control and management responsibility for the plan's administration and operation.[85] If the plan is a trust, it must also have a trustee who can be named in the trust instrument or appointed by the named fiduciary.[86] It is common in Taft-Hartley plans for the trustees to be the named fiduciaries.

A fiduciary under ERISA cannot generally delegate the responsibilities assigned it under the plan, although an important exception to this exists. The named fiduciary, if authorized to do so by the plan document, may allocate responsibilities to other fiduciaries so long as the delegation does not include "trustee responsibilities,"[87] for which separate rules apply.

The term *trustee responsibilities* refers to the trustee's responsibility to manage and control assets of the plan.[88] There are two rules, however, that do permit someone other than the trustee to manage or control assets. First, the plan instrument can provide that the trustee shall be subject to certain instructions of the named fiduciary (in which case the trustee is considered a "directed trustee").[89] Second, the plan instrument can permit the named fiduciary to appoint investment managers to manage or control plan assets.[90]

The investment manager must be a bank, a qualified insurance company, or an investment advisor under the Investment Advisors Act of 1940.[91] The investment advisor, who will have responsibility for managing some or all plan assets, must acknowledge in writing that he or she is a fiduciary. A named fiduciary will not be liable for the acts of a fiduciary to whom responsibilities were properly delegated, unless some other feature of the law is at play.[92] For example, the delegation itself must comport with fiduciary standards, and the

---

[84] Shaw v. IAM Pension Plan, 563 F.Supp. 653, 657 (C.D.Cal. 1983) (officials of employer are fiduciaries to extent they retain authority for selection and retention of trustees).

[85] ERISA § 402(a).

[86] ERISA § 403.

[87] ERISA § 405(c).

[88] Id.

[89] ERISA § 405(c)(3).

[90] ERISA § 402(c)(3).

[91] ERISA § 102(3B).

[92] ERISA § 405.

named fiduciary also has an obligation to periodically evaluate the delegees.[93]

The rules concerning delegation have obvious relevance to proxy voting. The Department of Labor, in a letter to the board chairman of Avon Products, expressed its view that it would be a violation of ERISA for either the trustee or the named fiduciary to cast proxies related to shares being managed by an investment manager appointed by the named fiduciary under the plan instrument (unless the named fiduciary "in developing such management responsibility to the investment manager . . . reserves to itself the right to vote proxies").[94]

ERISA subjects fiduciaries to four basic trust standards, each of which is discussed below. These are a duty of loyalty, found in a statutory exclusive benefit rule; a duty of prudence; a duty to diversify; and a duty to comply with the plan documents.[95] The legislative history indicates that Congress adopted these core trust principles, but with modifications appropriate to employee benefit plans. Several committee reports concerning ERISA counsel those charged with interpreting ERISA to "[bear] in mind the special nature and purpose of employee benefit plans."[96] (ERISA also includes specific trust-like reporting and disclosure requirements.)

The courts in fashioning a federal common law of pensions have often merged, and perhaps muddled, the statutorily distinct standards for fiduciary conduct. This may be explained, in part, by the fact that the different statutory standards emerged from the same bowl of primordial fiduciary soup. It may also be explained by the lack of sufficient statutory differentiation of the standards or by judicial lassitude. I nevertheless will discuss each statutory standard separately, noting in such discussions where courts have found overlap between standards.

---

[93] The ERISA Conference Report indicates that Congress expected that the named fiduciary would periodically review any delegee's performance. The report stated that "this requirement may be satisfied by formal periodic review, or it may be met through day-to-day contact and evaluation, or in other appropriate ways."

[94] Letter from Alan D. Lebowitz, deputy assistant Secretary of Labor, to Helmuth Fandl, chairman of the board, Avon Products, February 29, 1988, reprinted in 15 *Pension Reporter* (BNA) 376 (1988).

[95] ERISA § 1104.

[96] House Education and Labor Comm. Report on Employee Benefit Security Act of 1973, H. Rep. No. 93-533 (1973), at 11–12; Senate Labor Comm. Report on Employee Benefit Security Act of 1973, S. Rep. 93-127, 93d Cong., 1st Sess. (1973) 29.

Nonneutral Trustee

ERISA permits a plan sponsor to appoint an "officer, employee, agent, or other representative" as a fiduciary, including trustee.[97] This is consistent with trust law, which permits a settlor to choose its own trustee or even to appoint itself trustee. Given that Congress designed ERISA, at least in part, to protect employees from abuses by the sponsor, it is appropriate to speculate why ERISA countenances nonneutral fiduciaries, who will be tugged by their loyalty to the plan sponsor from the fealty required to the plan participants.

The legislative history provides no express answer, but there are at least three plausible explanations. The first is that Congress simply bowed to the reality that most employee plans had nonneutral trustees and administrators at the time ERISA was enacted. Requiring a neutral fiduciary would have created a new cottage industry and would have imposed additional costs on plan sponsors. It thus would have been difficult political going to mandate the use of neutral trustees; moreover, it seems evident that developing a structure for appointing neutral trustees would have been a formidable legislative undertaking, and ERISA gave Congress enough of those without adding the development of a mechanism to implement the neutral trustee requirement.

A second possible reason for the nonneutral trustee is that the private pension system is a voluntary system, and a neutral trustee requirement would have dissuaded at least some employers from adopting, or maintaining, pension plans. Professors Langbein and Fischel note that the disincentive would be particularly strong with respect to defined benefit plans, since the neutral trustee would be entrusted with benefit decisions that might increase plan costs and investment decisions that might decrease plan assets. Such decisions could increase future funding obligations and thus reduce future firm profitability.

A third possibility is that in granting license to the use of nonneutral trustees Congress was impliedly recognizing the plan sponsor's own beneficial interest in the trust, since nonneutral trustees by definition will have dual loyalties. This is the position developed by Professors Langbein and Fischel in the context of their argument that there are certain situations in which plan fiduciaries should legitimately be permitted to consider the employer's interests.[98]

---

[97] ERISA § 408(c).

[98] *ERISA's Fundamental Contradiction,* supra note 7.

The Duty of Loyalty and ERISA: The Exclusive Benefit Rule and the Rules on Prohibited Transactions

The trust-law duty of loyalty appears in two ERISA fiduciary sections: a statutory exclusive benefit rule and a series of specific prohibitions against transactions between plans and fiduciaries.

Prohibited transactions. The prohibited transaction rules cover five specific categories of self-dealing and also more generally prohibits self-dealing and conflicts of interest on the part of fiduciaries.

The specific prohibited transaction rules prohibit a fiduciary from causing a plan to enter into a transaction if the fiduciary knew or should have known that the transaction is effected with a party in interest. The specific proscribed transactions include sales, leases, and exchanges of property; loans; furnishing of goods, services, or facilities; transfers of plan assets; and plan acquisition of employer securities or real property in violation of statutory standards.[99] The more general prohibited transactions occur when a fiduciary deals with plan assets in his own interest or for his own account, represents a party in a transaction with the trust, or receives compensation from a party for a transaction with the plan.[100]

Parties in interest include all fiduciaries; service providers; employers; employee organizations; 50 percent owners of employers or employee organizations; certain relatives of other parties in interest; employees, officers, directors, and 10 percent shareholders of certain other parties in interest; corporations, partnerships, and trusts that are at least 50 percent owned by other parties in interest; 10 percent partners of other interested parties (except of fiduciaries).[101]

The rules on employer securities and real property prohibit a plan from acquiring any employer security or real property unless it is a qualifying security or property, which are defined terms. The plan may purchase qualifying securities or real property only if adequate consideration is paid, no commission is charged, and if immediately following the acquisition the aggregate fair market value of all employer securities and property does not exceed 10 percent of the value of the plan's assets.[102] This latter requirement does not apply to eligible individual account plans, which are profit-sharing, stock bonus, thrift, and

---

99 ERISA § 406(a).
100 ERISA § 406(b).
101 ERISA § 3(14).
102 ERISA § 407.

employee stock ownership plans (and certain pre-ERISA money-purchase pension plans) that expressly authorize the acquisition of employer securities or employer real property.[103]

ERISA includes other statutory exemptions from the prohibited transaction rules; it also authorizes the Department of Labor to grant either individual or class exemptions that are administratively feasible, in the interests of the plan and of its participants and beneficiaries, and protective of the rights of participants and beneficiaries.[104]

In addition, the Internal Revenue Code includes a parallel set of provisions, which impose an excise tax on "disqualified persons . . . who participate in a prohibited transaction (other than a fiduciary acting only as such)."[105] In terms of function, the nontax ERISA prohibited-transaction provisions include rules designed to prevent fiduciaries from permitting a plan to enter into prohibited transactions, while the tax rule penalizes disqualified persons who are on the other side of the bargain with the plan.[106]

Exclusive benefit rule. In addition to the specific proscriptions of the prohibited transaction rules, ERISA also requires fiduciaries to act for the exclusive purpose of providing participants and beneficiaries with benefits (and defraying reasonable administrative costs of the plan). The exclusive benefit rule is lifted from the LMRA's codification of the trust duty of loyalty. The Supreme Court, in *NLRB* v. *Amax Coal Co.*,[107] noted that ERISA made explicit judicial interpretation of the exclusive benefit rule under the LMRA:

> Other courts have similarly described the duty of loyalty under the ERISA, e.g., the duty to act with "complete and undivided loyalty to the beneficiaries of the trust . . . and with a single eye to the interests of the participants and beneficiaries.

The first issue concerning the exclusive benefit rule is whether it is only a general statement of the specific prohibited transaction rules and thus has no independent application. As a matter of statutory construction and legislative history, such an interpretation is certainly incorrect: It would reduce the language of the exclusive benefit rule to surplusage and, as already indicated, Congress seemingly envisioned the

---

[103] Id.

[104] ERISA § 408.

[105] I.R.C. § 4975.

[106] It is, of course, possible for the fiduciary who is responsible for a plan entering into a prohibited transaction to also be a disqualified person who was a party to the transaction.

[107] 453 U.S. 322 (1981).

general fiduciary provisions, including the exclusive benefit rule, to give rise to a body of federal common law for trusts. The prohibited transaction rules, however, are particularized loyalty rules, and there are probably few situations in which a court inclined to find a violation of the general rule could not also find a violation of a prohibited transaction rule, particularly the rules against acting for one's own account or for a third party, if a court were so inclined.

Courts, however, have not read these general prohibited transaction rules very broadly, perhaps to avoid creation of precedent for finding per se violations of ERISA any time a fiduciary acted in a way that benefited the plan sponsor. Courts thus have turned to the exclusive benefit rule in situations where a fiduciary took an action in which the fiduciary had an interest, such as where plan administrators have invested assets or used plan assets either to fight off a takeover bid or to effect a takeover by a company in which the plan administrator has an interest.[108] Note that these types of issues can emerge not only in plan investment decisions but also in the voting of shares.

These uses of the exclusive benefit rule have considerable overlap with the duties under the prudent man rule, since such investments often are made without appropriate investigation and care and are thus imprudent. In fact, courts sometimes turn to the prudent man rule in considering facts that seemingly raise loyalty questions. In some cases, however, a trustee's act arguably may be prudent but nonetheless offer such benefit to a fiduciary that analysis under the exclusive benefit rule becomes critical if we are concerned about ensuring the fiduciary's ability to act objectively as an aim or goal in itself.

Two approaches are possible: The first would be to require the fiduciary to delegate the decision to a neutral fiduciary; the other is to assess the propriety of the fiduciary's action by focusing on whether the fiduciary properly determined that his (or a third party's) interest was coextensive with the beneficiary's and thus any benefit accruing to the fiduciary was incidental. I will return to these choices, neither of which is without problems, in a later part of this section.

Langbein and Fischel argue that the exclusive benefit rule is the wrong standard for judging the actions of pension fiduciaries with respect to conflicts between classes of employees or between employees

---

[108] *See* Leigh v. Engle, 727 F.2d 113 (7th Cir. 1984) (fiduciary used plan assets in takeover bids by plan sponsor); Donovan v. Bierwirth, 680 F.2d 263 (2nd Cir. 1983) (plan assets used to fight takeover bid of sponsor; court refused to find per se violation of ERISA, relying instead on exclusive benefit rule). The *Bierwirth* case is discussed further in the text.

and the firm.[109] With respect to conflicts of employee interests, for example, the interest of younger employees in preserving their jobs as against the interests of older employees who will be more interested in the preservation of the fund's value, Langbein and Fischel would substitute a duty of impartiality for the exclusive benefit rule.

The more controversial part of their argument is that the exclusive benefit rule, at least if interpreted as incorporating a traditional trust-law duty of loyalty, forces courts to avert their vision from legitimate interests of the firm, interests that ERISA should recognize. Their argument begins from their observation that employee benefit plans are formed for complex reasons, which derive not only from employee goals, but also from goals of the firm. In enacting ERISA, Congress understood the legitimacy of these interests of the firm and recognized that the ability of the firm to effect these interests contributes to the willingness of the firm to sponsor employee plans.

Langbein and Fischel argue that in resolving disputes in which employer and employee interests collide, courts should abandon the exclusive benefit rule, as it has been understood to date, and instead determine whether recognition of the employer's interest "is consistent with the understanding that the employees and the employer would have reached had they bargained over the issue ex ante. Any other approach will lower the rate of plan formation," and will reduce the ability of the parties at the time of plan adoption to maximize value to the firm and the employees.

While I agree with Langbein and Fischel that a rule of impartiality is appropriate under ERISA for resolving participant conflicts that do not implicate employer interests, I have doubts that the ex ante bargain perspective is the proper one for resolving conflict between firm and employee. First, as a matter of statutory language, I think it difficult to conclude that Congress intended fiduciary action to be judged on such basis, notwithstanding ERISA's sanction of the nonneutral trustee and of reversions in defined benefit plans, which Professors Langbein and Fischel point to as explicit instances of ERISA recognizing employer interests. I would argue that such ERISA provisions were intended as specific rules rather than broad policy statements.[110] This view of the

---

[109] *ERISA's Fundamental Contradiction,* supra note 7.

[110] Langbein and Fischel observe, and I think correctly, that the ERISA rules permitting reversions are inconsistent with the application of the exclusive benefit rule to investments of defined benefit assets. Since the risk of such investments falls on the firm (and the PBGC), the employees' interest in investment selection is not as strong as that of the firm, at least in situations where the plan's assets are sufficient to cover

statutory language, however, is irrelevant to Professors Langbein and Fischel's broader policy argument, given the ability of Congress to amend ERISA's language.

Second, and more important, I have policy-centered concerns about the Langbein/Fischel approach. The first doubt is a practical one: courts are not well equipped to determine cases on the basis of a hypothetical bargain the parties would have struck had they foreseen the issue. In terms of permitting employee plan fiduciaries a measure of certainty in predicting how a court will resolve a dispute, a standard that asks what the parties would have agreed to ex ante does not seem to me more satisfactory than the exclusive benefit rule.[111]

The second doubt arises from my view that the exclusive benefit rule presently serves as a check on the action of nonneutral fiduciaries. It is such fiduciaries in the first instance who are faced with choices that implicate firm/employee conflicts. They, then, would be the decision makers who initially would have to decide what agreement the pension plan's parties would have reached ex ante. If they are interested decision makers, how are they to decide these questions objectively? Are they to act in an interested manner, since they are not neutral? Are they to guess how a court would decide the question *de novo*?[112] Or should a court ordinarily defer to their decisions? I would suggest that nonneutral decision makers simply cannot be entrusted with decisions pitting interests of the firm against those of the participants unless subject to a standard that probes decisions for self-interest. It is my view that, whatever its faults, the exclusive benefit rule is an

---

benefit obligations. *Cf.* Stein, *Raiders of the Corporate Pension Plan: The Reversion of Excess Plan Assets to the Employer,* 5 Am. J. Tax Pol'y 117 (1986) (arguing that ERISA should be amended to permit overfunded plans to invest surplus assets in employer securities). I am not certain, however, that by permitting reversions, Congress meant to announce a policy in which employer interests in pension assets should be recognized generally whenever the employer bears the greater share of investment risk. And at this conference, Assistant Secretary of Labor David Walker rejected this construction of the statute in response to questions following presentation of his paper.

Langbein and Fischel also observe that ERISA's license of the nonneutral trustee is inconsistent with the exclusive benefit rule. Langbein and Fischel thus conclude that Congress implicitly recognized that employer interests will be considered in making plan decisions.

I will return to each of these points in the text.

[111] Professors Langbein and Fischel recognize this, noting that "once recognized, the new standard will not transform fiduciary law from a hard field to an easy one. The issues in pension and welfare benefit plans will remain complex." *ERISA's Fundamental Contradiction,* supra note 7, at 94.

[112] To some extent, the doubts in this paragraph are a reframing of the doubts in the preceding paragraph, since a fiduciary would be called on to predict how a court would decide a question.

effective standard for policing discretion for self-interest (even if a sometimes costly rule where it prohibits the parties from maximizing value).[113]

The third doubt is that Professors Langbein and Fischel may undervalue certain participant interests, particularly in the upside performance of defined benefit investment assets. Professors Fischel and Langbein would argue that because risk in defined benefit plans generally incides on the firm, the firm should be permitted latitude in the use of plan assets for its own benefit. But despite investment risk nominally falling on the firm, employees may in fact share in both investment risk and investment gain. For example, a sour investment performance may cause the firm to recoup its losses by reducing future benefit accruals; investment performance in excess of actuarial assumptions may increase the probability that the firm will increase future benefit accruals. Such employee interest in investment performance may be especially keen in a system in which defined benefit promises are stated in nominal terms but mutual expectation is that benefits will be indexed to inflation.

This last doubt can be answered by noting that our laws have always permitted employers to terminate a pension plan and take a reversion and that our present law permits employers to remove assets from what is, in effect, an ongoing plan. Langbein and Fischel argue that if the law permits reversions, it should logically tolerate lesser interference with defined benefit assets, for example, voting stock to advance firm interests.

Here, I would acknowledge that reversions are inconsistent with the exclusive benefit rule, but argue that reversions are an aberration that should be addressed legislatively. Professors Langbein and Fischel do not share this view but believe that a prohibition on reversions would significantly lower the rate of plan formation (and thus would have adverse consequence for employees as a group). Thus, different views on the appropriateness of reversions may ultimately demarcate those who accept the exclusive benefit rule as wise policy despite its flaws from those who believe that the flaws consume the rule.

Notwithstanding the above-stated doubts about the standards Pro-

---

[113] It is possible that Congress adopted the exclusive benefit rule not only to maximize values to the plan sponsor and to the employee, but also to promote public confidence in the private pension system. It is of course true that some investments will serve both participant and sponsor interests (even some of the Teamster plan's joint ventures with the mob in Las Vegas apparently proved that crime can pay handsome returns to a pension plan), but that such investments undermine the confidence of the public in pension plans as a device to pay retirement income to workers.

fessors Langbein and Fischel propose to test fiduciary decision making, I do share their view that the firm has interests in the pension plan, some of which should override the exclusive benefit rule. I believe, however, that the policy considerations in making these decisions are too varied to entrust to a general standard, even one with as coherent a policy basis as that proposed by Langbein and Fischel.

Moreover, that standard seeks to identify hypothetical bargains the parties would have reached. Given that ERISA was enacted in large measure to interfere with market arrangements—to provide employees with protections they did not seem able to obtain in an unregulated market—I am not certain that the exclusive benefit rule is not the proper standard to judge fiduciary decisions, except where a specific contrary rule identifies an issue in which the employer's interest should prevail. In fact, ERISA does provide a number of exceptions to the exclusive benefit rule.

The most significant classes of such issues are those that have been identified as involving business rather than fiduciary judgments. These include the plan sponsor's decision to terminate a plan, to recover surplus assets, to select an investment philosophy or to select a funding method for a defined benefit plan, and to make "plan design" decisions, such as setting or adjusting benefit levels or determining which employees are eligible to participate in a plan. The prohibited transaction exemptions also identify an area in which the employer's interest should ordinarily prevail: where a neutral party—the Department of Labor—makes a determination that the interests of an interested party are not in conflict with those of the participants.

In effect, the exclusive benefit rule acts to prevent non-neutral trustees from making discretionary decisions that have a potential to advance the fiduciary's interests (other than a general interest in the plan's welfare). An unavoidable problem with the exclusive benefit rule, however, will arise when the firm has an interest that is either arguably not antagonistic to any employee interest or that is plausibly in harmony with the interests of at least some employees. In such situations, courts have attempted to evaluate whether any benefit to the fiduciary, or the plan sponsor who employs the fiduciary, was merely incidental and thus not the motivating factor for the decision.

In some cases, the incidental-benefit test does not seem especially troubling. For example, in the case of a profit-sharing plan that refuses a lump sum benefit to a former key employee to discourage key employees from leaving, competing with the employer, and thus reducing profits and plan contributions for other participants, the benefit to the remaining participants seems real, and the benefit to the employer is coextensive with the benefit to the participants.[114] Moreover, the former key employee does not lose his benefits; their payment is only deferred until retirement.

There are other decisions, however, where an incidental benefit test seems inappropriate because the fiduciary must take action, and the action taken will have such a marked effect on the welfare of the fiduciary (or a party related to the fiduciary) that his judgment is inherently suspect, and such an effect on the plan that the security of the participants is unequivocally threatened. Assume a hostile takeover bid and a fiduciary who is an employee of the plan sponsor where the sponsor is the target.[115] Assume also that some, or all, of the employees wish the takeover to be defeated because of concerns about job security and that actions taken to thwart the takeover bid thus will benefit plan participants.[116] It nevertheless would be difficult for the fiduciary to defend a promanagement stance as conferring only an incidental benefit on the plan sponsor or its management (i.e., that the decision was made to benefit the plan) unless the monetary return to the plan from acting in favor of management will exceed that of acting against management; moreover, asking a court to assess whether the benefit to the target was incidental or motivational is to ask a court to engage in judicial sorcery.

One much-discussed case, *Donovan* v. *Bierwirth*,[117] involved an attempt by LTV to acquire Grumman Corporation. The takeover was opposed by Grumman management, three of whom served as trustees for a defined benefit plan. The trustees determined that the plan would not tender the Grumman stock in its portfolio, even though LTV's offer exceeded the stock's trading price; moreover, the trustees caused the plan to invest in additional shares of stock (although not in excess of the 10 percent limitation that delineates the border of whether a pur-

---

[114] Courts have not been inconsistent in their resolutions of cases involving this issue. *Compare* Frary v. Shorr Paper Products, Inc., 494 F.Supp. 565 (N.D.Ill. 1980) (requiring plan to pay lump sum benefit) *with* Morse v. Stanley, 732 F.2d 1139 (2d Cir. 1984) (upholding plan decision to deny lump sum payment; benefit to firm only incidental). Professors Langbein and Fischel analyze the issue (in the context of *Morse v. Stanley*) by noting that at the time of initial contract the employer and employee share an interest in maximizing profit to the firm, and that a decision upholding plan action to deny payment of a lump sum benefit can be supported on this basis. On the other hand, Langbein and Fischel note that a plan's silence on the issue of whether lump sum payments are to be denied departing key employees makes the question more difficult.

[115] *See generally,* Note, *The Duties of Employee Benefit Plan Trustees under ERISA in Hostile Tender Offers,* 82 Col. L. Rev. 1692 (1982).

[116] This raises another issue: Should plan fiduciaries under ERISA be permitted to consider pecuniary social investing?

[117] 680 F.2d 263 (1982).

chase is a prohibited transaction). The Department of Labor argued that the trustee's actions were a violation of the general, anticonflict prohibited transaction rules.[118] The Second Circuit rejected this argument, holding that the only possibly relevant prohibition was that against representing a third party in dealing with the plan; here, Grumman was not a party to the transaction (the shares were purchased on the market), and the court held that the transaction fell outside the rule's proscription.[119]

The court then turned to ERISA's prudence standards. The court noted that "officers and directors do not violate their duties" by following "a course of action with respect to the plan which benefits the corporation as well as the beneficiaries," and thus adopted a legal standard that permitted employer fiduciaries to take action that they conclude "after adequate and impartial investigation," to "best promote the interests of participants and beneficiaries," even though such action "incidentally benefits the corporation."[120]

In its opinion, the Second Circuit suggested that the trustees, having committed themselves to opposing the takeover while standing in their corporate-officer boots, could not act objectively. The court suggested even more strongly that the trustees failed to satisfy their obligations under ERISA's prudence standard because the trustees failed to investigate adequately or give careful and impartial consideration to the merits of the actions they caused the plan to undertake. The court, however, seemed to limit the explicit basis on which it upheld the district court's preliminary injunction to the trustees' decision to purchase additional Grumman shares at a time when the market price for such shares was inflated because of the tender offer. The court found that such stock purchase put the plan in a "no-win" situation, since, if the tender offer failed (as appeared likely), the price of the stock would fall, and if the tender offer were successful, the plan would not want additional Grumman stock. Thus, "it [was] almost impossible to believe that the trustees . . . motive for purchasing the additional shares was for any purpose other than blocking the LTV offer."[121]

While the court did not expressly hold that a fiduciary automatically violates the exclusive benefit rule by failing to tender shares in a takeover in which a substantial premium over market price was offered, the court used language and reached a holding from which an inescapable message emanates: Interested fiduciaries are at great risk if

---

[118] Id. at 270.

[119] Id.

[120] Id. at 271.

[121] Id. at 275.

in a matter of importance they vote on the side of their interest. The court, then, seemed to use a standard that combined the deliberative duties of prudence with the more mechanical duty of loyalty.

Removing the profiduciary choice would hardly satisfactorily clarify policy, for generally this would mean uncritically tendering shares. This might, however, result in financial loss to the plan since the tender offer may not in fact represent fair value. Moreover, the employees may have a well-founded fear for their job security, and arguably this is an interest of which the plan fiduciary should take cognizance.

Perhaps a cautious ERISA fiduciary should, then, delegate these decisions to a neutral party, but on what basis is even a neutral fiduciary to make judgments?[122] May the fiduciary consider the effects of the takeover on the future job prospects of active-employee plan participants; on the sponsor of a defined benefit plan, who after all will be responsible for making up any funding shortfalls that a bad decision might create and who is entitled to any surplus assets on plan termination; on the economy generally? Or should we confine such a neutral fiduciary to questions of monetary return to the plan (but in a takeover situation what should the fiduciary do with respect to an overfunded defined benefit plan in which the increased return will accrue to the benefit of the acquiror)? Perhaps the fiduciary should toss hard questions to the participants through expanded pass-through voting.

There are, then, two issues raised by these hard questions: first, whether we should entrust a decision maker with a discretionary role when the decision maker's own interests are vitally affected and possibly in conflict with at least some of the plan's participants; second, regardless of who makes decisions, what standards should be used in determining whether a decision serves the exclusive benefit of the participants?

Selecting appropriate standards requires broad policy judgments that, in my view, are not properly resolved by fiduciaries, by the Department of Labor, or by courts, on a case-by-case basis, at least not given the talisman Congress has fashioned as a guide. I would suggest that these decisions are legislative in nature and would be best resolved by Congress enacting specific rules.

Prudent Man Rule

ERISA incorporated the prudent man rule of trust law, but with a twist. The *Restatement of Trusts* defines the prudent man rule as follows:

---

[122] There would also be a question of whether the decision could be delegated under the plan instrument.

> In making investments of trust funds the trustee is under a duty to the beneficiary . . . to make such investments and only such investments as a prudent man would make of his own property having in view the preservation of the estate and the amount and regularity of the income to be derived.[123]

ERISA modifies this standard by setting as the standard "a prudent man acting in a like capacity and familiar with such matters . . . ."[124] This standard adds flexibility to earlier formulations by permitting fiduciaries to consider the special nature of employee benefit plans; it also permits fiduciaries to consider the needs of the particular plan for which they have responsibility—the size of the plan, the need for liquidity, the type of plan, the ages and characteristics of the employees, etc.

Perhaps the most important departure of the ERISA prudence rule from the trust rule is the deemphasis on each particular investment. Recall that under trust law each plan investment may be subject to objection if imprudent; thus, certain investments, such as speculative securities, were illegal per se. In fact, most states had legal lists of some sort, which identified proper trust investments (except for trusts whose governing document varied the ordinary trust-law requirements). ERISA, however, has no legal lists, and prudence is judged by the anticipated performance of the total portfolio given the needs of the plan. In fact, the preamble to the Department of Labor's regulations on prudence indicates that venture capital and precious metals may be appropriate investments for some plans.[125]

The regulations themselves indicate that a fiduciary satisfies the prudent man rule if he has given appropriate consideration to all appropriate facts or circumstances that the fiduciary knew or should have known were relevant to the investment and its role in the plan's total portfolio, and then acts in accord with such consideration.[126] Relevant considerations include the composition of the portfolio, the portfolio's liquidity, and the portfolio's projected return. It should be stressed that the prudent-man standard under ERISA is satisfied through the development of, and fidelity to, a procedure of judging investments. These procedures should include adequate investigation of investments and alternatives, and also consultation with appraisers, accountants, bankers, lawyers, and other experts when appropriate.

Another important distinction between the ERISA formulation of

---

[123] *Restatement of Trusts Second* § 22.

[124] ERISA § 403(a)(B).

[125] 44 Fed. Reg. 37225 (June 26, 1979).

[126] 29 C.F.R. § 2550.404a-1(b)(1).

the prudence rule and the trust-law formulation is that trust law was concerned with "the preservation of the estate and the amount and regularity of the income to be derived," while the ERISA standard is concerned with liquidity and total return of the plan's portfolio. The trust standard's concerns with income and preservation of the estate to a large extent reflect the concern of protecting both the income and remainder beneficiaries, whose respective interests were determined by the common law's distinction between principal and income. This concern is not so relevant to pension plans, which generally pay benefits from their total assets.

As we have already seen, the Second Circuit in *Donovan* v. *Bierwirth* putatively used a prudence standard in evaluating the propriety of actions that arguably violate a duty of loyalty as well. This in part follows naturally from the procedural orientation of the prudent man rule: Consideration of improper factors infects the process by which investment decisions are reached. It also reflects, I think, a determination by some courts to avoid laying down inflexible principles for judging loyalty: The prudent man rule is shrouded in oracular blurriness, thereby permitting courts latitude to do right by their lights in particular cases without creating rules with a capacity to haunt in later cases.

The prudent man rule is sometimes raised as a bar to social investing; the Department of Labor has taken the position that a prudent man will not sacrifice return for social objectives. But the department has apparently permitted plans to invest with an eye toward social goals if the investment is considered economically equivalent to other available investments. For example, the Department of Labor has granted a prohibited transaction exemption permitting investments in construction loans for plan sponsors, and at least one court has permitted a fund to contract with firms using union labor (which the Department of Labor challenged).[127] One difficulty for plans with social investing objectives is that the task of screening acceptable investments adds transaction costs; it is my understanding that plans that attempt to realize social objectives with their investments will usually do so only after documenting that additional transaction costs are trivial.

We generally think of the prudent man rule as a standard for judging investments of plan assets, but in ERISA, which reduces fiduciary standards to four rules, the prudent man rule should also apply to other uses of plan assets, including proxy voting. The question of how to vote shares of stock is subject not only to a loyalty standard, but also a prudent man standard. The Department of Labor has taken this posi-

---

[127] Donovan v. Walton, 609 F.Supp. 1221 (S.D.Fl. 1985), *aff'd sub nom.* Brock v. Walton, 794 F.2d 586 (11th Cir. 1986).

tion. Former Secretary of Labor Brock stated in a 1986 speech that "[w]ith regard to corporate governance, plan fiduciaries cannot be passive shareholders. Specifically, proxy votes that may affect the economic value of plan investments unquestionably involve the exercise of fiduciary responsibility. Those votes must be cast in a way that a fiduciary believes will maximize the economic value of plan holdings."[128]

A common and heated example of the problems of proxy voting is found in management proposals for prophylactic defensive measures against hostile takeover bids. What are a fiduciary's obligations in such a vote? Is it enough to have procedures that investigate how to vote shares? If so, what criteria should be used in deciding to vote? One might argue that defensive measures are always inimical to the shareholders, and, if this view were taken, plan fiduciaries would always be required to vote against such measures. One might argue in response that in some cases defensive measures will free management to run the company without concern about fending off takeover bids, or that such measures protect shareholders either by coercing higher bids or by preventing two-tier offers that may be unfair to initially nontendering shareholders. I suspect, however, that when a fiduciary votes for a poison pill or other defensive measure, there are other pressures being brought to bear (for example, a corporate fiduciary who has some connection to the corporation proposing a poison pill).

Questions also arise outside the sphere of corporate defensive measures. What, for instance, are a fiduciary's options when deciding how to vote (or whether to tender shares) when an unaffiliated company is approached by a suitor who proposes a merger favorable to existing shareholders but whom the fiduciary believes will take action inimical to the employees (such as terminating the pension plan or laying off employees)? It can be argued that at least in the case of stock in the plan sponsor, such considerations should be considered by the plan fiduciaries; in other cases, such action could only be justified if the fiduciary believes that the long-term prospects of the target company outweigh the benefits of the market premium being offered for the shares by the raider or if we are willing to countenance social voting of shares.

There are also the pure social voting situations: how should a fiduciary vote on a question concerning whether a company should continue doing business in South Africa? If such votes will reduce the value of the firm, at least on a short-term basis, does the trustee act

---

[128] Remarks of Secretary of Labor William Brock, Annual Meeting, Association of Private Pension and Welfare Plans, Washington, D.C. (1986).

imprudently in casting such votes? The Department of Labor position seems to be an apparent yes.

Questions also arise where there is a contested election for seats on the board. Must a fiduciary investigate each contested election? Such investigation would be expensive and burdensome. Can the investigative function be delegated under the fiduciary rules? Would plan pooling of investigative resources be considered a delegation on the part of each participating plan? Finally, what would the economic and social implications of a pooling arrangement be? The power to decide how institutional investors vote in proxy battles is a considerable power indeed.

Duty to Diversify

ERISA requires plans to diversify investments "so as to minimize the risk of large losses, unless under the circumstances it is clearly prudent not to do so."[129] This is essentially the standard under the *Restatement of Trusts:* The trustee must diversify unless he can prove that under the circumstance it would not have been prudent to do so.[130] A significant difference between trust law and ERISA, however, is that the diversification requirement cannot be waived by the settlor in ERISA trusts, except in certain defined contribution plans designed to be invested primarily in employer stock.

Given the different types of employee plans, Congress believed it could not develop rules that stated the diversification rules with numeric certainty; thus, the duty to diversify is stated in general language. But ERISA's legislative history does indicate the following factors that should be weighed by a fiduciary in assessing whether an investment will violate the diversification rules.

1. Purpose of the plan.
2. Amount of assets involved in the investment.
3. Financial and industrial conditions at the time of investment.
4. Diversity of type of investment.
5. Geographic and industrial diversity.
6. Maturity dates of bonds.[131]

---

[129] ERISA § 404(a)(1)(C).

[130] *Restatement of Trusts Second* § 228.

[131] Conference Report 304.

The legislative history indicates that plans can satisfy diversification requirements by use of pooled asset funds, if after investigation it appears to the fiduciary that the asset fund is diversified.

Courts have found diversification requirements to have been violated when a plan invested 23 percent of assets to a single real estate loan,[132] and also when a plan had invested 81 percent of its assets in real estate projects, even though they were varied in type.[133]

The Arbitrary and Capricious Standard and Benefit Claims

ERISA authorizes participants and their beneficiaries to bring actions for benefits. It also requires fiduciaries to act in accordance with plan documents and the exclusive benefit rule, which also have application to benefit claims.

In the section of this paper on trust principles that were applicable to pension plans, I concluded that unless the plan documents provided otherwise (which most pension plans did), a trustee should have been required to treat benefit questions as contractual in nature when the interests of the plan sponsor and the plan beneficiary collide. I also noted, however, that in benefit cases arising under the LMRA, courts generally judged trustee action using an arbitrary and capricious standard.

Nothing in ERISA's legislative history, however, purports to adopt the judicially crafted arbitrary and capricious standard. Thus, ERISA included no mandate for the arbitrary and capricious standard. Moreover, ERISA has a specific participant enforcement provision for challenging fiduciary action[134] and as noted, a provision permitting participants to sue for benefits.[135] If ERISA considered a benefit denial a fiduciary rather than a contractual question, there would have been no need for a separate provision authorizing actions for benefit claims, since the fiduciary enforcement provision would have provided jurisdiction for benefit claims.

Nevertheless, the great majority of courts have adopted an arbitrary and capricious standard for assessing the propriety of benefit denials. There has emerged, however, a minority view that the arbitrary and capricious standard permits less deference "where . . . the employer's

---

[132] Marshall v. Glaziers Pension Plan, 507 F.Supp. 378 (D.Haw. 1980).

[133] Donovan v. Mazzola, 2 EBC 115 (N.D. Cal. 1981).

[134] ERISA § 502(a)(1)(C).

[135] ERISA § 502(a)(1)(B).

denial of benefits to a class avoids a very substantial outlay" on the part of the employer.[136] In a recent Seventh Circuit case, Judge Posner called for a flexible arbitrary and capricious standard that would increase in rigor as the employer's interest in the benefit decision became more substantial.[137]

More recently, the Third Circuit, in *Bruch* v. *Firestone Tire & Rubber Co.*[138] held that the proper standard of review for benefit denials is a contractual one if the fiduciary has a conflict of interest. In such a case, the presumption of impartiality that the arbitrary and capricious standard presupposes is simply not appropriate. The Third Circuit rejected Firestone's argument that deference should be accorded to the fiduciary's decision, since the fiduciary had expertise as a claims administrator. The court noted with respect to the argument that the decision turned on a contractual question, a type of question to which courts do in fact bring expertise. "Courts have no reason to defer to private parties to obtain answers to these kinds of questions."[139] The Third Circuit decision, which includes a historical analysis of how the arbitrary and capricious standard came to be employed in ERISA, indicated that the standard is more appropriate to Taft-Hartley trusts, where the trustees are balanced between management and union; in other words, where the trustee can be expected to act impartially.

The Supreme Court has granted certiorari in *Bruch* v. *Firestone Tire & Rubber Co.*

Role of the Department of Labor

An important aspect of ERISA is that it authorizes the Secretary of Labor to bring actions respecting fiduciary violations.[140] Trust law authorized government officials to bring actions only in the case of charitable trusts. ERISA did, however, identify strong governmental interests in pension trusts, and such trusts are in one sense charitable. Here it is interesting to observe that in 1919 the Bureau of Revenue granted

---

[136] Jung v. FMC Corp., 755 F.2d 708 (9th Cir. 1985).

[137] Van Boxel v. Journal Co., 836 F.2d 1048 (7th Cir. 1987).

[138] 828 F.2d 134 (3d Cir. 1987), *cert. granted,* 108 S.Ct. 128 (1988). In *Firestone,* the employer maintained an unfunded salary continuation plan. Firestone sold a plant, and the plant's employees contended that the plan applied to them (even though most of them continued to be employed by the purchaser). If the plan did apply, Firestone would bear the cost. Because of this interest on the part of Firestone, the Third Circuit held that the proper judicial standard review was one based on contractual principles.

[139] Id. at 144.

[140] ERISA § 502(a)(2).

tax exemption to pension trusts on the ground that they were charitable in nature.[141]

It should be noted that the Department of Labor has authority to challenge fiduciary actions even though those actions were approved by a majority of participants.

Reporting and Disclosure

ERISA requires plans to report to both the various governmental agencies and to plan participants.[142] ERISA's legislative history indicates that periodic and adequate disclosure is necessary if participants and the Department of Labor are to police the actions of plan officials for violations of the fiduciary standards.[143] Among the information that is made available to the government agencies are accountants' reports; the assets held for investment; fiduciary information, including transactions between the plan and parties in interest; transactions involving more than 3 percent of the plan's assets; and in defined benefit plans, actuarial information.[144] Participants are entitled to benefit statements; summary plan descriptions; and by request, copies of the latest annual report; any terminal report; the bargaining agreement, the trust agreement, contract, or other instruments under which the plan is operated.[145]

The required disclosure under ERISA may provide access to less information, and fewer documents, than a trust beneficiary would have been entitled to under trust law. This raises a question of whether a pension plan participant can use the general ERISA fiduciary requirements to gain access to information not available in the plan annual reports and other documents to which he or she does have automatic access.

An issue that is now before the Supreme Court in *Firestone* v. *Bruch*[146] is whether a former employee is a participant in the plan for purposes of requesting information from the plan.

---

141 O.D. 110, 2–19–165, 1919 C.B. 224.

142 ERISA, Title I, Subtitle B, Part 1.

143 *See, e.g., H. Rep. No. 533,* supra note 76, at 11; *S. Rep. No. 93–127,* supra note 76, at 27.

144 ERISA § 123.

145 ERISA § 124. The plan administrator may charge participants for information that is available only on request.

146 828 F.2d 134 (3d Cir. 1987), *cert. granted,* 108 S.Ct. 128 (1987).

Spendthrift Clause

ERISA requires plans to include clauses against a participant assigning or transferring interests, with two statutory exceptions:[147] If an employee is in pay status, he or she may revocably assign 10 percent of a benefit payment; an employee can borrow using his plan interest to secure the loan.

Involuntary assignments have raised more difficult questions. Courts were particularly sympathetic to the claims of former spouses, much as they had been under non-ERISA trust law. Congress in 1984 enacted legislation that permitted assignment of interests to former spouses who are granted a "qualified domestic relations order," which has a number of conditions, including that payments cannot be made prior to the participant's acquisition of the earliest retirement age under the plan.[148] Courts have also struggled to mesh the bankruptcy laws with the ERISA spendthrift clause, but a detailed accounting of that struggle is not within the ambit of this paper's topic.

SUMMARY OF ISSUES IN THE APPLICATION OF TRUST LAW TO PENSION PLANS

The foregoing discussion should suggest that the task of applying trust law to pension plans was a complicated undertaking before ERISA and remains one after ERISA. There are two reasons for this: Trust law provides only general guideposts for judging fiduciaries generally, and pension plans are complicated arrangements around which the interests of many parties are in orbit and sometimes collision. In this section, I will abstract from the preceding discussion factors inherent in pension plans that tend to complicate the application of trust principles.

The first problem is identifying who are the trust settlors and beneficiaries. Earlier in the paper I indicated that nominally the plan sponsor—the employer or employer and union—are settlors, and the employees are the beneficiaries. The reality of the relationships in a pension plan, however, belies the seeming ease with which we snap to judgment. In fact, the employees might be considered the settlors of the plan, since they presumably sacrifice cash wages to pay for the employer's contributions to the plan. (One could take issue with this statement: How, for instance, do we explain reversions if the employees are the settlors? Reversions, however, can be explained on two grounds,

---

[147] ERISA § 206(d); 401(a)(13).

[148] ERISA § 206(d)(3); I.R.C. § 401(a)(13)(B).

neither of which negates the employee settlor function. First, the employees are cosettlors with the plan sponsor with the employer being the settlor party entitled to the reversion; second, the employer sells an insurance product to the employees, that is, the value of each year's benefit accrual, with the employer accepting investment risk and thus reserving the right to investment surplus.)

There is another arguable settlor: the government. Most pension plans subject to ERISA are tax-favored (i.e., the government contributes to the plan through effective reduction of the tax burden of the pension-plan parties). Moreover, the government is a settlor in another sense through its charter of the PBGC. The PBGC, to the extent it provides insurance coverage of underfunded plans at below-risk rates, is contributing to the plan to the extent of the value of the coverage over true market premiums for the coverage.

Since in traditional trust law we look to the settlor for instructions (and we continue, to some extent, to do this under ERISA), the very fact of three settlors whose interests are not necessarily in sync complicates resolution of issues.

We can turn the multisettlor perspective on its head and perhaps see the same three parties—employer, employee, and government—as beneficiaries of the plan, all with their own interests. To an extent, however, this depends on our view of what constitutes a beneficial interest in a pension plan. Certainly the only party entitled to actual retirement benefits is the employee, although in defined benefit plans the employer may have an interest in plan surplus. Related to the interest in a defined benefit surplus is the employer's interest in maximizing plan return either to reduce future contributions or to increase a revertible surplus. But the employer has other interests as well, such as the plan's ability to engender employee loyalty, to reduce turnover, to encourage superannuation of older employees and to satisfy moral yearnings to provide loyal, long-time employees with the dignity of an adequate retirement income. The government too has interests, the most apparent of which is the protection of the PBGC, but only slightly less evident is the subsidy of retirement savings, thereby relieving the state from some of its welfare burden.

Another complicating factor, already alluded to, is that contributions to a pension plan generally are continuing, which is not ordinarily the case with other trusts. Parties that share the economic responsibility of making such contributions have a deeper stake in the plan's continuing welfare; this is especially the case with defined benefit plans, where actions that sacrifice optimal financial returns for other goals will increase the funding burden of the responsible parties.

It is too often reflexively assumed that the employer bears the risk of poor return and of capital losses. It is possible that the employer has the ability to pass a part of such losses to the employee-participants, either by reducing wages, future benefit accruals, or other concessions. Richard Ippolito's study of reversions from defined benefit plans suggested that employers have the ability to impose, at least on a one-time basis, capital loss on the employees (through terminating a plan indexed to final pay, and funded on an indexed basis; on plan termination, only nominal benefits are paid).[149]

The government may also bear plan losses, if not directly through the PBGC, then indirectly through the diminution of the retirement benefits the government hoped to purchase through the tax benefits.

The inquiry on whom loss falls is a significant one, for it will give us some guidance on who should be permitted to impose risk on the plan through social investing or proxy voting. My suggestion that the employees may in fact bear some of the risk of loss in a defined benefit plan, notwithstanding that the loss nominally falls on the firm, suggests that perhaps the employees should have some voice in how shares are voted or where money is to be invested even in defined benefit plans. The suggestion that the government bears loss also casts some doubt on the notion that there are few policy constraints on defined contribution plan participants casting proxies on a basis other than optimizing return to the plan.

Related to these questions is whether plan fiduciaries should be able to consider any factors other than maximizing plan return. As we have seen in this paper, such considerations abound: Employees may wish to invest in the employer, or fight a takeover, in order to preserve jobs for plan participants; or lend money to plan participants to enable them to purchase personal residences; or invest in firms that use union labor. Using plan assets for each of these purposes may be in the interest of plan participants, but is it an interest that a plan fiduciary should be permitted to consider?

This leads us to another problem: Participants have differing interests. Younger employees may place less value on a future pension than older employees. Moreover, older employees in defined benefit plans or target benefit plans will receive accruals of far greater value than younger employees. Younger employees, however, may be willing to take risks with pension assets if those risks may yield greater job security. In nonparticipant-directed defined contribution plans, the trade-off of yield for job security will fall directly on all plan participants. This may not be so with respect to defined benefit plans, if the plan will

---

[149] Ippolito, *Issues Surrounding Pension Terminations for Reversion,* 5 Am. J. Tax Pol'y 81, 96–98 (1986).

continue through the retirement of older employees, regardless of low returns, or if the benefit levels do not exceed PBGC guarantees.

There may also be conflicts between active employees and retirees, since retirees generally will have little interest in trading return for job security. On the other hand, if a plan terminates, ERISA forces initial allocation of plan assets to participants who have been (or could have been) in pay status for three years, and it is therefore unlikely that many retirees will suffer investment loss directly. But in the past many plans have used extraordinary, and inflation-induced, investment gains to fund ad hoc benefit increases. If a plan trades optimal returns for other goals and benefits, it is improbable that a plan will grant such increases. This raises a further question, however: Are retirees entitled to such increases? Under present law they are not, but there are signs that the law might ultimately yield to requiring such increases in certain situations (such as plan terminations).[150] More pertinent, however, is a different question: Should plans be required to design their portfolio to make such increases probable?

Finally, there is the problem that Professors Langbein and Fischel believe is central to understanding ERISA's fiduciary requirements: the express sanction of the nonneutral trustee. Should this fact of ERISA life cause us to rethink the exclusive benefit rule, to accord recognition to certain employer interests even when in conflict with employee interests? Or is the presence of the nonneutral trustee and its built-in bias the factor that should cause courts to apply the exclusive benefit rule with unyielding rigor, even though such application may have an adverse effect on plan formation?

PROXY VOTING, LOYALTY, AND PRUDENCE

We have seen that the trust duties of loyalty and prudence, and perhaps impartiality, are the standards by which a fiduciary's voting of shares must be tested. In this final section of the paper, I identify situations in which a conflict of trust norms with fiduciary voting behavior might occur. Because of its overlap with voting of shares, I will also note takeover situations involving not voting, but tendering of shares.

We should note at the outset that voting issues can arise in three types of settings: first, those that involve how a plan will vote shares in the plan sponsor; second, those that involve how a plan will vote shares in a company other than the plan sponsor, but on an issue that

---

[150] Last term bills cleared the Senate Labor Committee and the House Education and Labor Committee that would have given a portion of a plan's termination surplus to retirees and active participants.

will have an effect on the plan sponsor, the plan participants, and beneficiaries, or the plan fiduciary; third, those that involve how a plan will vote shares in a company other than the plan sponsor on issues that do not have an actual effect on any party to the pension plan.

1. *Morally Oriented Voting.* A fiduciary might be faced with a dispute in which the plan sponsor, the beneficiaries, or even the trustee, wish to trade optimal return for other benefits that might be of a moral nature, for example, not investing in the defense industry or in tobacco or alcohol companies, in firms that are perceived to have an animus toward organized labor, and so forth. Some governmental plans have cast votes on moral grounds, particularly with respect to divestment in firms doing business in South Africa.[151]
2. *Pecuniary Objectives Other than Maximization of Return to Plan.* A plan might hold stock in a corporation that the plan sponsor is attempting to cause to take certain business actions. For example, a union might wish a plan to vote its utility stock interests for directors committed to causing the utility to purchase union coal, as in the *Blankenship* case.
3. *Attempted Hostile Takeover of Plan Sponsor.* Defensive use of plan assets might reduce the value of the stock of the plan sponsor, but management and perhaps the plan participants wish to prevent the takeover.
4. *Attempted Takeover by Plan Sponsor.* Use of plan assets to acquire shares or vote shares in a company that the plan sponsor is attempting to acquire.
5. *Plan Sponsor and Shark Repellants, Poison Pills, and So Forth.* The plan sponsor may wish to adopt certain measures designed to make the plan sponsor less attractive as a takeover target.
6. *Neutral Fiduciaries.* A bank or other corporate entity might serve as investment manager for a plan. Such entities may have a business relationship with companies in which the plan has a holding. Conflict situations that parallel those identified with the plan sponsor can arise.
7. *Takeovers and Defensive Measures in Firms with No Plan Affiliation.* May the firm consider factors other than ultimate return to the plan? For example, may the firm ask whether a hostile takeover will result in loss of jobs to workers (which

[151] *See* The Biggest Lump of Money in the World (1986).

would bring this situation into the morally oriented voting category of issues)? Can a plan fiduciary take the position that takeovers generally are unhealthy for the economy and will have an adverse effect on the overall holdings of the plan? Or must a vote be based simply on maximization of value to the plan? And if so, can the plan consider long-term prospects of the firm under current management even if the current market price does not fully reflect such prospects?

8. *Stock Options to Employees of Plan Sponsor.* Certain qualified stock options require vote of shareholders.
9. *Election of Plan Sponsor's Directors.*
10. *Voting of Shares in ESOP.* The extent of holdings of some ESOPs are extensive enough to swing a proxy fight. Participants are given pass-through voting rights for shares allocated to their account if the stock is required to be registered under section 12 of the Securities Exchange Act; for closely held corporations, the rules are less demanding. Even pass-through voting has been criticized, since management may have too great an influence on participants and many participants may not vote at all.
11. *Voting on Incumbent Management of Portfolio Company.*

CHAPTER 2

ERISA Proxy Voting in the Real World

by

George W. Cowles*

To further understanding of how ERISA trustees handle proxy voting, this paper outlines the proxy voting process as it exists at one major institution, for actively and passively managed discretionary accounts and for so-called directed accounts. The paper also discusses the process when a plan sponsor wishes to get involved in the voting of proxies on the securities held in its plan's portfolios, as well as the notion of pass-through voting and the special considerations surrounding the voting of proxies on employer securities held in individual account defined contribution plans.

STRUCTURE

In order to understand how the proxy voting process works within a major financial institution that handles a number of ERISA accounts, it is necessary to understand in what capacity the institution is acting for individual accounts. Banks can, and do, act as trustee, agent for individual trustees, custodian, and/or investment manager for ERISA accounts. As an investment manager, banks also can actively manage the account or can passively manage the account, through index funds.

As trustee, agent, or custodian, the bank may be one of several investment managers or may act merely in a "directed" capacity, meaning that someone else actually exercises investment discretion over the assets. For instance, in the typical master trust arrangement, common

* Senior Vice President, Bankers Trust Company.

among large ERISA plans today, the bank, acting as master trustee of the several individual portfolios comprising the master trust, may or may not exercise investment discretion over one or more of the portfolios. Others, such as investment advisory firms, insurance companies, other banks, or the plan sponsor itself (all referred to as the *investment manager*), manage the portfolios. In this case, the bank is often referred to as a *directed trustee*. This implies that the investment manager (or managers) tells the trustee which securities to purchase or sell within the portfolio. In practice, however, the entity exercising investment control deals directly with a broker of its choice with respect to purchases and sales and directs the trustee to settle the transactions it has entered into on behalf of the trust account.

THE PROXY VOTING PROCESS

In ERISA accounts today, it is almost a universal practice for the proxies on equity securities to be voted by the entity that exercises investment discretion. If the trustee has investment discretion over a portfolio of equity securities, it is responsible for voting the proxies with respect to those securities. On the other hand, if the bank is acting as a directed trustee, the proxy voting authority, and responsibility, rests with the entity that has investment authority over the securities. In the latter situation, it is common practice for the directed trustee to execute (i.e., sign and date) the proxy card in blank and forward it to the investment manager, the entity with proxy voting authority. Since the directed trustee is the owner of record of the security, only the directed trustee can sign the proxy card to make it valid.

On receipt of a validated proxy card, the investment manager votes or abstains on each issue as it sees fit and returns the proxy card directly to the issuer or proxy solicitor. The card is *not* returned to the directed trustee. Bankers Trust management knows of no cases where a directed trustee asks investment managers for instructions on how to vote proxies on shares over which they have proxy voting authority and then votes the proxies as directed. Proxies are voted by the entity exercising investment discretion in much the same way as securities are purchased and sold. The directed trustee's involvement in the process is merely to execute the card in blank in order to validate it.

When a bank exercises investment discretion over an ERISA account that contains equity securities, whether as trustee or investment manager, it votes the proxies on those securities. The most common practice for carrying out proxy voting authority within a bank is for a committee to make the decision as to how each proxy shall be voted. Usually the bank has developed a written policy statement for guidance in the voting of the various issues that may appear on any given proxy. Such policy statement may indicate, for example, that routine proxy items such as the uncontested election of directors or the appointment of auditors are to be voted as management of the issuer recommends, and that nonroutine proxies are to be referred to the appropriate investment research analyst for review. In the latter case, the analyst would then make a recommendation to the responsible committee with respect to each nonroutine issue on the proxy. Generally this procedure would be followed on proxies on all equity securities, whether held in actively or passively managed portfolios. As a result, banks that provide passively managed products, such as expanded universe index funds, may be voting as many as 3,000–4,000 proxies a year!

PLAN SPONSOR INVOLVEMENT IN PROXY VOTING

Much has been written and said about the trend of the ERISA plan sponsor community's growing involvement in the proxy voting process. In Bankers Trust experience such involvement has been, and continues to be, infrequent. In those few cases where a plan sponsor may be involved, there are several levels of involvement. Some plan sponsors have issued proxy voting guidelines to their investment managers. Such guidelines may include a directive to the manager to vote all proxies and to vote them solely in the interest of plan participants. The guidelines may include other guidance as well. The issuance of proxy voting guidelines has increased since the Department of Labor released a letter in February of this year detailing its views on proxy voting.

The next level of plan sponsor involvement in the proxy voting process includes those very few sponsors who have issued guidelines and requested that their investment managers notify the sponsor in advance when the manager intends to vote against the issuing company's management. In our experience in these instances, there has been absolutely no sponsor pressure on how any vote should be cast. When informed in advance, the sponsor's response has been, "Thank you very much for the information."

In even fewer situations, a plan sponsor may take back from its managers, or retain, proxy control either partially or in total. There are those who believe that in this situation the trustee is directed how to vote by the plan sponsor and, therefore, is co-responsible for the vote. On the contrary, these rare situations are structured so that the underlying documentation makes it clear that the sponsor (named fiduciary) has retained unto itself the right to vote proxies. Procedurally, the trustee will execute the proxies in blank in these cases and forward them to the named fiduciary, which will then vote the proxy and send it directly to the issuer or proxy solicitor. Thus, the trustee has no responsibility or co-responsibility for a vote that has been cast by the named fiduciary—the trustee has merely validated the proxy card for the use of the named fiduciary in the exercise of its undelegated responsibility.

PASS-THROUGH PROXY VOTING

There are those who advocate the notion that proxies on equity securities held in all ERISA funds should be voted by the beneficial owners of such securities, that is, the plan participants. Although this is an interesting concept, there appears to be only two ways in which it could be accomplished—actually passing the proxy voting through to the participants or having a committee comprised of a representative group of participants (including retirees) assume proxy voting responsibility. In the author's view, neither alternative works. Actual pass-through voting fails on a practical and economic basis, and the committee approach is likely to fail in practice.

Consider, for instance, the potential costs of passing the proxy voting responsibility through to plan participants. If the cost of producing a set of proxy material, mailing it to the participant, and providing a postage-paid return envelope costs $2; if the average ERISA account holds 100 equity securities; and if there are 50 million participants; the cost of the pass-through would be $10 billion ($2 × 100 × 50,000,000). This is a very considerable expense to be borne, even by the trillion dollar private pension system. The second problem with pass-through voting on a market basket of equity securities is ignorance and apathy. Using the above assumption of an average of 100 securities per fund, each participant would be required to review, to understand the issues, and to vote on all these proxies. The author doubts that the return from participants would be more than 1 percent. The use of expanded universe index funds that may hold upwards of 1,500 equities would lower the rate of return to almost nothing.

The committee of representative participants approach to proxy voting has some appeal on its face. Here too, however, the issues of ignorance and apathy surface. The author is aware of one situation in which this approach was used, and it was eventually abandoned. The principal reason for abandonment was that employees who were appointed to a three-year term on the committee invariably asked to be relieved of the assignment within a few months. When asked why, the responses included one or all of the following reasons: "I don't understand the issues"; "I don't feel I can represent my constituents"; "It takes too much time away from the job I'm paid to do"; "I do not feel competent to do the job." Again, consider the expanded universe index fund in this context, and it will be apparent why the author feels that the committee approach is impractical.

PROXY VOTING OF EMPLOYER SECURITIES

The one area where pass-through voting works well is with the proxies on equity securities of the plan sponsor held in defined contribution plans, such as ESOPs, 401(k) plans, or thrift plans. Although probably not a universal practice, it is extremely common for employee participants to vote the proxies on the shares of employer securities credited to their accounts under these plans. Cost is not a significant issue. Apathy is not a factor since the issuer is the participant's employer. Neither is ignorance an issue since participants are well informed about their employer and well aware of the issues and problems it faces. Concern over coercion of participants by management is often expressed, but in the author's experience, coercion does not take place. Even if it were to occur, virtually all plans specify that the participant's instruction to the trustee as to how his shares are to be voted is confidential. How participants vote is not disclosed to anyone except in bulk numbers, that is, "*X* shares yea," "*Y* shares nay." Proxy voting clearly is an incident of ownership, and in the case of employer securities in a defined contribution plan, participants are demonstrably the owners of specific numbers of shares. In this case, pass-through proxy voting is practical, and it works.

There are only five alternatives to the voting of proxies on employer securities in these plans—(1) the right to vote the proxies is passed through to the participants; (2) the trustee votes the proxies; (3) the named fiduciary (plan sponsor) votes the proxies; (4) a fiduciary (ies) independent of all parties votes the proxies; or (5) the proxies are not voted by anyone. Not having the shares voted may lead to a lack of a quorum; the trustee may have a conflict of interest in some situations with his client, the plan sponsor; the named fiduciary may have a conflict of interest; there are public policy and legal issues that arise out of the sponsor voting his own shares; and no one seems to like the idea of totally independent fiduciaries. In short, pass-through is the answer.

One thorny issue remains in this limited pass-through voting situation—how the shares for which no participant instructions are received shall be voted. Alternatives include the following: the trustee votes, the named fiduciary votes, an independent fiduciary (ies) votes, the shares are not voted, or the shares are voted in the same proportion as the shares for which instructions are received.

In Bankers Trust's experience, the virtually universal practice is to vote undirected shares in the same proportion as shares for which instructions are received. The plan specifies this practice, and it is followed. For reasons enumerated above, proportional voting works while other alternatives for voting undirected shares probably will not work. This procedure causes the shares to be voted as willed by a random sampling of the owners. If any constituency's vote is leveraged by the process, it is that group who, because the vote is confidential, will vote against management on all issues merely to vent their collective spleen.

Pass-through voting on employer securities is appropriate and practical and should continue. Perhaps the answer to those who challenge the practice is an amendment to ERISA to require pass-through voting in this area. After all, there is precedent in the law and regulations surrounding ESOPs where pass-through voting is required.

CHAPTER 3

Fiduciary Obligations of the Plan Sponsor with Regard to Proxy Voting

by

Hazel A. Witte, Esq.*

Robert N. Sandler, Esq.†

One of the primary duties of shareholders is to hold management accountable for its actions by either selling their stock or by exercising their choice on proxy resolutions. As investment dollars in the equity market increase, corporate officers and policymakers have turned their attention to the potential of pension plans to act as shareholders.[1]

The role of institutional shareholders, particularly pension plans, has been emphasized by the expanding visibility of public plans, which have sponsored shareholder resolutions and actively campaigned against management-entrenching proxy issues. There has even been public discussion of pension plan representation on boards of directors. Given the role of boards in takeover fights, their capacity for that role, and the increasing frequency of legal challenges to board decisions from shareholder suits, the role of pension funds as large shareholders, in theory, encompasses almost all facets of corporate decision making.

---

* Assistant Chief Counsel, *Benefits Policy,* Office of Advocacy, U.S. Small Business Administration.

† Reinhart, Boerner, Van Deuren, Norris & Rieselbach, P.C. The opinions expressed in this paper are those of the authors only.

[1] Employee Benefit Research Institute (EBRI) Quarterly Pension Investment Report, 1st Quarter 1988, p. 9. Equity assets of private trustee funds totalled $430 billion in equity out of total assets of $1.191 trillion. Total financial assets for 1987 amounted to $1,037.4 trillion for private trustee plans, and $521.4 billion for state and local plans. QPIR, p. 42.

THE PUBLIC REVIEW

Policymakers have thus far limited their examination of pension funds as shareholders to proxy voting activity, that is, whether proxies were being voted in the best interest of the plan participants, and whether those responsible for voting proxies were diligently carrying out their responsibilities. Policymakers were uncertain as to how and whether proxies were being voted. Congressional hearings on pension plans by both the Subcommittee on Oversight, Senate Governmental Affairs Committee,[2] and the Subcommittee on Telecommunications and Finance, House Energy and Commerce Committee,[3] and many recent pronouncements by the Department of Labor (DOL), concentrated on institutional investors as shareholders, and made it clear that the treatment of proxies by institutions, particularly pension plans, was somewhat suspect. Policymakers presumed it necessary to emphasize that proxies were to be treated as full-fledged plan assets, and that voting was serious business.

As the role of pension funds as shareholders became fully appreciated during the takeover battles of the past few years, instructions for voting proxies and opportunities for pressure to affect the voting behavior were publicly scrutinized. The Senate hearings, in particular, led to a recommendation that the Employee Retirement Income Security Act of 1974 (ERISA) be amended to require that independent fiduciaries be retained to vote the plans' proxies under certain circumstances. Another recommendation was that the DOL issue a policy statement regarding the obligations of pension fund fiduciaries.[4]

LEGAL BACKGROUND OF PROXY VOTING

When one is considering the fiduciary obligations of the sponsor of an employee benefit plan with regard to the voting of proxies appurtenant to shares of stock held by the plan, it is helpful to first consider the legal background. A good place to begin is with Section 402(a) of ERISA,[5]

---

[2] *Pension Funds in the Capital Markets.* Hearings before the Subcommittee on Telecommunications, Consumer Protection, and Finance, 99th Congress, 2nd Session, March 19, 1986.

[3] *The Department of Labor's Enforcement of the Employee Retirement Income Security Act.* Hearings before the Subcommitee on Oversight of Government Management, 99th Congress, 1st Session, June 25 and 26, 1985.

[4] *The Department of Labor's Enforcement of the Employee Retirement Income Security Act.* A Report Prepared by the Subcommitee on Oversight of Government Management, 99th Congress, 2nd Session, April 1986.

[5] Public Law No. 93-406,93rd Cong, 2nd Sess. (Sept 2, 1974).

which states that all plans must identify one or more "named fiduciaries" in the plan documents, which persons are given the authority to control and manage the operation and administration of the plan.

In addition, Section 403(a) of ERISA provides that the plan trustee either be named in the plan document or be appointed by the named fiduciary. The trustee has the exclusive authority and discretion to manage and control plan assets. There are, however, two exceptions. The first exception is when the plan trustee is directed by a named fiduciary. Any such direction must be in accordance with plan documents and not in violation of any provisions of ERISA. The second exception exists when the named fiduciary has delegated fiduciary authority and responsibility to investment managers under Section 3(38) of ERISA. Only named fiduciaries and not trustees may delegate their duties to investment managers.

Section 404 of ERISA requires a fiduciary to discharge his duties prudently, in accordance with plan documents, and for the exclusive purpose of providing benefits to participants and defraying plan expenses. Under Section 404 regulations,[6] the exclusive benefit rule is satisfied if a fiduciary (1) has given appropriate consideration to those facts and circumstances that the fiduciary knows or should know are relevant to the particular investment or investment course of action involved and (2) has acted accordingly.

Section 404 of ERISA prohibits certain transactions between plans and "parties in interest" as defined in Section 3(14) of ERISA and also prohibits acts of fiduciary self-dealing. Parties in interest must pay an excise tax of 5 percent of the amount involved in a prohibited transaction under Section 406 of ERISA, and fiduciaries may be personally liable under Section 409 of ERISA for plan losses that result from a breach of their fiduciary duties.

AVON LETTER CONSIDERATIONS

In a letter to Avon Products dated February 23, 1988, the DOL stated that "in general, the fiduciary act of managing plan assets which are shares of corporate stock would include the voting of proxies pertinent to those shares." Therefore, the full panoply of fiduciary duties, as described above, applies to the voting of proxies. Blindly following management under the "Wall Street Rule" would not, in the view of the DOL, discharge a fiduciary's duties.

The DOL provides an example in the Avon letter whereby a pro-

---

[6] 29 CFR Section 2550.404a-1.

posal to change the state of incorporation of a company could affect the value of a plan's investment in that company if, for instance, the laws of the new state were less favorable regarding shareholder rights. Another example of a decision having economic impact is a vote to rescind a poison pill arrangement. A key question is where the line should be drawn as to whether proxy issues have an economic impact.

The DOL concluded in the Avon letter that if discretionary authority has been delegated to an investment manager, the named fiduciary may not direct the investment manager or improperly pressure the investment manager with regard to proxy voting. Such direction or pressure may result in a violation of the fiduciary duties of both the named fiduciary and the investment manager.

The DOL did state that trustees are permitted to accept directions from named fiduciaries. As a result, it would appear that named fiduciaries may delegate general discretionary authority to an investment manager, keep proxy voting authority with the trustee, and direct the trustee with regard to proxy voting. However, such arrangements would be closely scrutinized by the DOL for improper directions. The DOL also stated in the Avon letter that those charged with voting proxies must analyze proxy voting decisions having an economic effect on the plan's investment and reduce their analysis to a written report.

In a general information letter sent to Theron Frye, dated February 16, 1982, the DOL was asked whether a proposed transfer of voting common stock held by a plan for nonvoting stock that was represented to be identical in value would violate the prohibited transaction and fiduciary responsibility provisions of ERISA. The DOL noted that one of the purposes of switching to nonvoting shares was to prevent a shift of control and that the appraiser had not valued the relinquishing of voting rights. The DOL stated that even if adequate consideration were paid, the acquisition of nonvoting shares for voting shares might violate the exclusive purpose rule of Section 404(a)(1) of ERISA if the primary purpose of the exchange was to prevent the plan from gaining voting control of the employer.

The Avon letter has raised a number of questions that private plans should answer for themselves if the proxy vote has economic value and is a plan asset:

1. If the plan sponsor provides direction on how to vote the proxy to the investment manager (including independent investment advisers, insurance companies, and trust departments of banks), is it proper?

2. If direction on a specific proxy vote is provided and the plan sponsor loses its insulation from fiduciary responsibility, what are the consequences?

3. If the vote is directed, what should be included in the report to assure that a violation of fiduciary duty did not occur, and that voting was done solely in the interest of the participants and beneficiaries?

4. How should the plan monitor investment managers to make sure proxies are voted, and, if plan guidelines exist, voted in accordance with such guidelines?

SUBJECTS AND ISSUES THAT MAY BE SUBMITTED FOR SHAREHOLDER APPROVAL

Assuming that the voting of proxies does generally have economic value and involves fiduciary acts of management of plan assets, what are the duties of plan fiduciaries charged with the responsibility of voting such proxies? In answering this question, it would be useful to review the types of subjects and issues that are or may be submitted for shareholder approval. Since a majority of Fortune 500 companies are incorporated in Delaware, the following comments on state shareholder approval issues are limited to Delaware law.

Amendments to the certificate of incorporation must be submitted for shareholder approval and include the following: (1) change in the state of incorporation; (2) change in authorized capital stock, for example, adding a new class of stock or increasing or decreasing the number of authorized shares; (3) limiting director liability; (4) "fair price" provisions requiring a formula payout to shareholders in the event of a change in control; (5) staggered or classified board of directors; and (6) a super-majority voting requirement for fundamental changes.[7]

The board of directors has the authority to select auditors, amend bylaws, adopt poison pills and shareholder rights plans, and enter into contracts between the company and its officers or directors. However, a number of companies submit such actions to shareholders for their approval as a policy matter.

What are the options of dissenting shareholders? Under Section 262 of the Delaware Corporation Law,[8] shareholders can demand an appraisal of the value of any class or series of stock of the corporation with regard to a merger or consolidation. The rules are complicated and require in general, that (1) the dissenting shareholder neither voted in favor of, nor consented in writing to, the merger or consolidation; (2) a separate written demand for the appraisal of shares has been made; and (3) the shareholder must have held the shares from date of vote to the effective date of merger or consolidation.

---

[7] Del. Code Ann. Tit. 8, Section 242 (1983).

[8] Del. Code Ann. Tit. 8, Section 262 (1983).

In addition, a shareholder may institute a derivative action, pursuant to which he must own shares of stock in the company and demand or demonstrate the futility of a demand of the action he deems appropriate. The suit is brought on behalf of the corporation, charging directors or officers with injuring the corporation as a result of breach of corporate fiduciary duty.

Section 14 of the Securities Exchange Act of 1934 (the "Exchange Act")[9] provides that it is unlawful to solicit any proxy with regard to any security registered under Section 12 of the Exchange Act in contravention of such rules and regulations as the Securities and Exchange Commission (SEC) prescribes. Rule 14a-8 under the Exchange Act sets forth guidelines for shareholders to make proposals in a company's proxy statement. In brief, the proponent must own at least 1 percent or $1,000 in market value of securities of the company and must have held such securities for at least one year. There are limitations on proponents who deliver proxy materials to holders of more than 25 percent of the company's stock, making it difficult for institutional investors attempting to rescind poison pills.

A proposal to be presented at an annual meeting must be received by the company not less than 120 calendar days in advance of the date of the company's proxy statement released to shareholders in connection with the previous year's annual meeting. A proponent may submit no more than one proposal with a supporting statement not to exceed 500 words.

A company may omit a proposal from its proxy statement if:

1. The proposal is not a proper subject for action by shareholders.
2. The proposal would require the company to violate any state or federal law.
3. The proposal is contrary to any SEC proxy rule, including the prohibition against false or misleading statements in proxy soliciting materials set forth in Rule 14a-9.
4. The proposal relates to the redress of a personal claim or grievance.
5. The proposal relates to operations accounting for less than 5 percent of the company's total assets.
6. The proposal deals with a matter beyond the company's power to effectuate.
7. The proposal deals with the matter relating to the conduct of the ordinary business operations of the registrant.

---

[9] 17 U.S.C. Section 78a.

8. The proposal relates to an election of an officer.
9. The proposal is counter to a proposal to be submitted by the company at the meeting.
10. The proposal has been rendered moot.
11. If the proposal is substantially duplicative of a proposal previously submitted to the company which is included in the company's proxy material for the meeting.[10]

As a result of the above, there is substantial latitude for institutional investors to place proposals in proxy statements; however, companies also have substantial latitude in rejecting such proposals. And, investors must pay their own bills for expenses related to printing and circulation of their proxies. In the past, investors were mostly passive and rarely objected to management proposals, let alone made proposals of their own. Now, there is a totally new environment as institutional investors begin to flex their considerable muscle. Both companies and investors will become increasingly familiar with the details of Rule 14a-8 and their respective state corporate law regarding shareholder rights.

In various pronouncements, the DOL has made it clear that not all votes involve a fiduciary act. As an example, uncontested votes on items such as appointments of administrative service providers can and in many instances should be delegated to proxy voting services. This would not be deemed a delegation of fiduciary authority to manage and dispose of plan assets.

ANTITAKEOVER RESOLUTIONS

In response to the furious pace of merger and acquisition activity in recent years, it is not surprising that a substantial portion of Fortune 500 companies have adopted antitakeover or poison pill measures. In a recent EBRI Issue Brief,[11] it was noted that more than one half of the Fortune 500 companies voted to create a classified board of directors, and more than 75 percent of the companies authorized the issuance of blank check preferred stock, giving management the ability to issue an unlimited number of shares. Nearly half enacted some type of "golden parachute," providing top executives with substantial benefits in the event of a takeover and the loss of the executive's job.

In general, poison pill arrangements need not be approved by

[10] Rule 14a-8 under the Securities Exchange Act of 1934, 17 C.F.R. Section 240.14a-8 (1987).

[11] EBRI Issue Brief No. 70, September 1987.

shareholders, although there has been a substantial increase in the efforts of institutional investors to remove poison pills. In the May 2, 1988, *Pensions and Investment Age*, it was reported that shareholders at United Technologies Corporation, Allied-Signal, Inc., and Consolidated Freightways, Inc., voted down the first of more than 20 antipoison pill resolutions. The State of Wisconsin Investment Board sponsored the resolutions at United Technologies, which is 54 percent owned by institutions, and at Allied-Signal, which is 50 percent owned by institutions. The California Public Employees' Retirement System sponsored the resolution at Consolidated Freightways, 76 percent of which is institutionally owned.

The votes in favor of the antipoison pill resolutions ranged from a low of 32 percent to a high of 45 percent. The SEC has derailed efforts by International Paper, Dayton-Hudson, and Upjohn to keep antipoison pill resolutions sponsored by institutional investors off their 1988 proxy statements. The Teachers Insurance and Annuity Association-College Retirement Equities Fund is sponsoring the International Paper and Dayton-Hudson antipoison pill resolutions.

In justifying the adoption of antitakeover measures, corporate management normally emphasizes their responsibilities beyond maximizing shareholder wealth. They argue that raiders have only short-term profits as a goal. Institutional investors, on the other hand, are often opposed to antitakeover proposals, since several studies have suggested that such measures, particularly poison pills, may tend to reduce stock prices.

CONGRESSIONAL ACTIVITY

Congress is now considering legislation sponsored by Senator William Proxmire and reported out by the Senate Banking Committee. The purpose of the Tender Offer Disclosure and Fairness Act[12] is to improve disclosure and protect shareholders against market manipulation and abuses perceived in the tender offer process. Several provisions of the bill apply specifically to pension plans, including one provision which would amend ERISA to prevent the use of surplus assets in a defined benefit plan to finance, directly or indirectly, the purchase or repayment of loans made to acquire a target employer's securities. Employee shareholders could, however, use the pension surplus to launch a bid for the company.

[12] Tender Offer Disclosure and Fairness Act of 1987, S.1323, introduced by Senator William Proxmire (D-Wis.) on June 4, 1987. Companion bill is H.R. 2577.

In addition, the bill would clarify that in voting on a merger, sale, or tender offer, a fiduciary is to take into consideration the long-term as well as the short-term interests of participants and beneficiaries of the plan. This provision is intended to clarify that a fiduciary is not necessarily required to accept the highest bid for shares owned by the plan if the long-term interests of participants and beneficiaries would be better served by holding the stock.

The bill would also require that owners of more than 10 percent of a company can, at the company's expense, include their own proxy materials and candidates for the board of directors in the proxy mailing distributed by the company. This provision of the bill is viewed as enabling large institutional investors to play a more active role in the management of the company and in choosing those who will run the company.

Representative John Dingell has introduced the Tender Offer Reform Act of 1987,[13] which is designed to ensure all players a level playing field in takeover situations without inhibiting bona fide tender offers. The bill restricts greenmail and golden parachutes; shortens the 10-day reporting period to disclose stakes of 5 percent or more; lengthens the tender offer period from the current 20 business days to 60 business days; mandates one share, one vote; and restricts poison pills.

Congress recently enacted the Competitive Quality Banking Act of 1987 (CQBA).[14] Congress perceived a threat by so-called nonbank banks to more traditional full-service, small independent banks and savings and loan institutions, and placed restrictions on the acquisition and formation of banks by nonbanks. Nonbanks are grandfathered with regard to banks they controlled when the law was enacted. To maintain the grandfather, there are limits placed on how much stock they may "control" in other banks and thrifts. They are deemed to have such control if they or their affiliates have discretionary authority to vote clients' bank stock proxies. If the right to vote is deemed shared with the client, such stock is not attributed to the manager for CEBA grandfather purposes.

While only a limited number of institutions qualify for the grandfather, they tend to be some of the largest institutional money managers in the country. As a result, sponsors should be cognizant of CEBA restrictions on certain of their managers, since such managers will want to "share" proxy voting responsibility with the plan trustee or named fiduciary.

---

[13] Tender Offer Reform Act of 1987, H.R. 2172, introduced by Representative John Dingell (D-Mich.) on April 27, 1987.

[14] Competitive Quality Banking Act of 1987 Public Law No. 100-86, 100th Cong., 1st Sess. (August 10, 1987).

CONSEQUENCES OF PUBLIC POLICY REVIEW OF PROXY VOTING PROCESSES

Plan sponsors and investment managers are now grappling with the wisdom of taking back the vote. Management is far more interested in the institutional investors' stake in their companies than they were during the first set of congressional hearings by the Senate Committee on Oversight. Mergers and acquisitions accentuate the value of a plan's holdings in a company that is either a takeover target or object of shareholder dissatisfaction. Though there is no formal move by plans to take back the vote, there is plenty of interest in presenting the implications of the Avon letter to investment boards and boards of directors.

Acceding to pressure to vote with management rather than in the best interests of plan participants and beneficiaries violates the strictures of fiduciary duty. The EBRI survey of plan sponsors and investment managers found that pressure on plans voting internally was rare and that external managers did not fare much worse. When they experienced pressure, those groups were more likely to have written policies that dealt with the issue of pressure.[15]

Where there is a threat of takeovers, management may make their desires known that plan sponsors should carefully review the wisdom of their votes and that voting with management on shareholder resolutions is in the best interest of the plan participants. DOL policies do not preclude all communications from companies in which voting stock is held, including the plan sponsor's company. However, the violation of the exclusive benefit rules may subject fiduciaries to enormous liability, and it is this potential liability that may govern behavior.

In a situation where the plan sponsor takes back the vote and leaves other investment decisions intact for investment managers, it will be difficult to rebut accusations of conflict once they arise. If the proxy vote has economic value and is a plan asset, who is better able to vote than the party making the decision to buy the stock? The buying party is best able to know the management of the company and has expectations of the stock that may be partially influenced by the outcome of the proxy vote. It is questionable that the plan sponsor would have any more flexibility to cast the vote given the standard of the exclusive benefit rule.

Linking the delegation of proxy voting to the delegation of other key elements of the investment process may also link proxy voting in a plan sponsor's scrutiny of overall performance. If appropriate proxy voting guidelines and procedures reduce the chance of exposure to

[15] *See* Footnote 8.

liabilities, they have their place in the overall evaluation of investment managers by plan sponsors.

WRITTEN POLICIES OF PLAN SPONSORS

There is now more pressure on both plan sponsors and investment managers to have written investment policies overall, and guidelines for proxy voting, in particular. Plan sponsor guidelines may range from the very broad, for example, all proxies must be voted in the interest of the plan participants, to far more specific, including the following:

1. All proxies must be voted, and generally voted with management unless disadvantageous to the plan; although management may normally be supported on all noncontroversial issues.
2. Guideline 1 above, with the addition that social and political issues without precedent are to be voted by the entire committee; and social and political issues with precedent are to be voted as before, unless reconsideration is needed.
3. Guidelines 1 and 2, with the addition of support for shareholder resolutions that takeover defenses be submitted to a vote and support for management on issues involving an increase in stock with a specific purpose, limiting director liability, adoption of options, and employee stock ownership plans. In addition, a vote on the merits should be required with regard to staggered boards, super-majority provisions, poison pills, adoption of classes of securities with different voting powers, and shareholder actions.
4. Guideline 1, with the addition that investment managers should vote against antitakeover resolutions in order to maximize investments as long-term investors; however, conversely, resolutions that have the effect of entrenching and benefiting management are not to be supported.

Any of these guidelines could be supported, as long as they are applied consistently. Departing from the guidelines could call into question whether the plan sponsor has adhered to the exclusive benefit rule.

CONCLUSION

As stated above, plan sponsors are generally named fiduciaries and, as such, are charged with ultimate fiduciary responsibility for monitoring the proxy voting procedures of those with discretionary authority to vote proxies. Recent cases and DOL pronouncements have emphasized the importance of "procedural prudence." The manner in which fiduciaries make decisions is deemed almost as significant as the substantive basis and result of such decisions. The courts have stated that named fiduciaries may themselves be liable for the imprudent investments of an investment manager.[16]

It is imperative, as a result, that named fiduciaries: (1) be fully cognizant of their duties, obligations, and potential liabilities under ERISA with regard to proxy voting; (2) review current guidelines and procedures regarding such duties and obligations; and (3) implement appropriate measures to rectify any current problems and to assure future compliance.

---

[16] Dardaganis v. Grace Capital, Inc., 8 E.B.C. 1939 (S.D.N.Y. 1987).

CHAPTER 4

Fiduciary Obligation of the Plan Trustee

by
Lawrence K. Cagney, Esq.*

INTRODUCTION

The question of who votes securities owned by an employee benefit plan has received a great deal of attention recently.[1] The significance of this question can only be measured by assessing the power that such plans, as a group, hold over corporate America. While the market crash may have caused plans to shift significant assets from equity investments, public and private pension plans still have over $500 billion invested in actively managed equity assets.[2]

The size of such holdings has not gone unnoticed in the corporate board room. The concern over "who votes the stock" is a direct outgrowth of the realization that pension plan investors can assist management in obtaining its goals and enhancing its security and that plan investors systematically opposed to certain management programs can destine any such program to failure. For these reasons, during 1987, many chief executive officers lobbied their counterparts at other corporations to exert pressure on the managers of such other corporations' pension funds to adopt programs that would block takeovers.[3]

---

* Associate, Debevoise & Plimpton, New York City.

[1] *See, e.g., The Proxy Pressure's On,* Pens. & Inv. Age, September 21, 1987, p. 3, col. 1; *Companies Tighten Control over Proxy Vote,* Pens. & Inv. Age, May 4, 1987, p. 4, col. 1; *Managers Pressured to Change Proxy Votes,* Pens. & Inv. Age, September 29, 1986, p. 1, col. 1.

[2] *Equity Market Exodus,* Pens. & Inv. Age, February 8, 1988, p. 1, col. 1.

[3] *Proxy Battles Heating Up,* Pens. & Inv. Age, April 6, 1987, p. 1, col. 1; *CEOs Lobbied for Pension Votes in Favor of Anti-Takeover Plans,* Pens. & Inv. Age, March 9, 1987, p. 1, col. 3.

Such lobbying has greatly concerned the Department of Labor. Directions from a corporate officer to the investment adviser of the corporation's plans may violate the provisions of the Employee Retirement Income Act of 1974, as amended (ERISA), governing the responsibilities of fiduciaries and precluding certain transactions with, or for the benefit of, certain parties related to a plan (such as the employer sponsoring the plan). For this reason, the department had been seeking a test case with respect to proxy voting[4] and investigated at least one corporation whose chairman had been openly supportive of a corporate role in the voting of plan-owned securities.[5] In its review of proxy voting with respect to that corporation's pension plan, the Department of Labor could not conclude that any fiduciary violation had occurred. However, because of the recurring nature of the issue of who votes securities held by a plan, the department issued a letter to that corporation's retirement committee (and its pension plan's investment managers) "to apprise you of the department's views concerning the general fiduciary obligations of a named fiduciary and an investment manager appointed pursuant to Section 402(c)(3) of ERISA with respect to the voting of proxies on plan-owned stock."[6]

The purpose of this paper is to address the issues arising under ERISA with respect to proxy voting, with particular emphasis on the implications of these issues with respect to the independent trustees of qualified employee benefit plans. The paper will not address situations in which corporate officers or other related individuals (e.g., majority shareholders) serve as trustees of a plan. Such related trustees may vote securities owned by the plan unless the authority to vote the securities has been delegated to an investment manager (as discussed below). However, the related trustees also face conflicts of interest that cause problems under ERISA beyond the scope of this paper. While the analysis in this paper is generally applicable with respect to individuals who serve as trustees, the focus is directed at commercial institutions that serve in such capacity.

The paper first explores the basis for applying the fiduciary responsibility provisions of ERISA to decisions regarding proxy voting. It then

---

[4] *Executives Warned of Proxy Vote Liability,* Pens. & Inv. Age, May 18, 1987, p. 1, col. 1.

[5] *See U.S. Warns Companies Not to Influence Proxy Voting of Pension Fund Managers,* The Wall Street Journal, February 29, 1988, p. 4, col. 2. For a discussion of Avon's chairman's publicly stated position on this issue, *see Avon Fighting Short-Term Emphasis,* Pens. & Inv. Age, April 20, 1987, p. 1, col. 1.

[6] Letter from Department of Labor to chairman of the Retirement Board of Avon Products, Inc., dated February 28, 1988, *reprinted in* BNA Pension Rpt., vol. 15, no. 9, 391 (February 29, 1988) (hereinafter referred to as *DOL Letter*).

addresses who is the proper fiduciary to exercise such fiduciary authority and notes the significant differences between the responsibilities of a trustee and an investment manager with respect to proxy voting, with emphasis on the problems confronted by a trustee subject to the directions of a named fiduciary. Finally, the paper discusses the question of liability in the context of proxy voting and whether directing proxy voting is itself a prudent decision.

PROXY VOTING AS A FIDUCIARY DECISION

To determine whether, and to what extent, ERISA's fiduciary responsibility provisions apply to the voting of securities owned by a plan, one must first determine whether, and to what extent, the exercise of the right to vote such securities is a fiduciary decision. Actions that require the exercise of discretionary authority to acquire or dispose of assets of a plan or that involve discretionary control over or management of such assets are subject to the fiduciary responsibility provisions of ERISA; actions that are merely ministerial or administrative are not fiduciary actions.[7] Thus, the primary question is whether voting securities owned by a plan is a ministerial function or one involving the exercise of discretionary authority.

The most important factor in determining whether the right to vote is a fiduciary decision would appear to be the nature of the issue being decided by shareholders. The power to vote securities on an issue that essentially involves the acquisition or disposition of plan assets—such as approving a merger or a recapitalization—is a fiduciary decision because it involves the exercise of discretionary investment authority. Such a vote will have a direct effect on the value of the securities being voted and may affect the form of securities or other property held by the plan.

Where the decision being made by shareholders has no direct economic effect on the company's securities, it is not as clear that a decision as to how such securities are voted involves an exercise of discretionary investment authority. However, if a decision regarding issues that have an indirect effect on plan-owned securities does not involve an exercise of investment discretion, it is likely that a fiduciary could not justify a vote that might limit the short-term value of the plan's securities, such as a vote for a management incentive plan that dilutes the plan's interest or a poison pill defense that might restrict potential purchases of the plan's securities. A fiduciary who votes in favor of

---

[7] 29 U.S.C. § 1003(21); *see also* 29 C.F.R. § 2509.75–8.

proposals, such as a compensation plan that has a dilutive effect on the plan's interest or a program designed to keep a company independent, may only do so without violating ERISA by concluding that the purpose and effect of such programs—to provide current management with meaningful incentives and a secure working environment—will enhance the value of the company and hence the plan's securities, over the long term. Thus, votes on matters that have an indirect financial impact on the plan's interests are likely fiduciary decisions.

A vote on an issue that is essential to the operation of the company but has little or no effect, direct or indirect, on the value of a plan's securities—such as the appointment of independent accountants—does not appear to involve any investment decision. Voting on such an issue is akin to having one's car inspected—it's an important ongoing operational activity done once a year with little thought or concern about its consequences. It may be argued, however, that even a vote involving such operational activities may involve a fiduciary decision because the right to vote securities is a right attached to a plan asset and exercising that right involves the exercise of the discretionary authority to manage and control plan assets. While the primary basis on which a person is determined to be a fiduciary is the power to acquire or dispose of plan assets, a person may be a fiduciary by reason of having discretionary management and control over plan assets.[8]

The Department of Labor apparently agrees with such an argument. Under the above analysis, any vote that may be exercised with respect to a plan-owned security involves a fiduciary decision, regardless of the issue being presented to shareholders. The Department has stated that "[t]he fiduciary act of managing plan assets which are shares of corporate stock would include the voting of proxies appurtenant to those shares of stock" and any decisions as to how such proxies should be voted "are fiduciary acts of plan asset management."[9] Thus, the Department of Labor would appear to believe that every vote, regardless of the issue presented, is a fiduciary decision.

WHICH FIDUCIARY VOTES THE PLAN'S SECURITIES

Assuming that the Department of Labor is correct that voting securities owned by a plan is always a fiduciary act, the question becomes which fiduciary has the responsibility to vote such securities. Subject to certain limitations and restrictions, ERISA expressly permits the allocation of authority among fiduciaries.

---

[8] 29 U.S.C. § 1003(21).

[9] *DOL Letter, supra* note 6, at 392.

ERISA generally requires that the assets of an employee benefit plan be held in trust, except to the extent that such assets are invested in insurance contracts.[10] If the assets are held in trust, but for two exceptions, the trustee must be given discretion over the investment of the trust's assets. The two exceptions are where the named fiduciary of the plan has reserved the authority to direct the trustee as to the proper investment of all or a specified portion of the plan's assets or has appointed an investment manager within the meaning of Section 3(38) of ERISA to manage all or a specified portion of such assets.[11] With respect to these two situations, the trustee retains title to the assets, but investment decisions are made by another fiduciary. The trustee is required to carry out such decisions and directions, provided that the requisite appointments or directions have been made in accordance with the provisions of ERISA (a trustee without discretion shall hereinafter be referred to as a *directed trustee*).[12]

The named fiduciary of a plan may, therefore, allocate fiduciary responsibilities among itself, the plan's trustee, and any investment manager it appoints. Thus, in theory, a trustee could hold securities acquired for a plan, while an investment manager has discretion over the decision to acquire or dispose of such securities, and the named fiduciary has the authority to determine how such securities are to be voted. Whether this could actually be accomplished depends on whether the plan and its ancillary documents, including the trust agreement, permit the named fiduciary to provide for such an allocation of fiduciary responsibility.[13]

Ultimate responsibility for the investment of plan assets rests with the plan's named fiduciary. The named fiduciary must be identified in the plan document or through procedures set forth in the plan document.[14] As noted above, the named fiduciary may either permit the trustee to exercise discretion, appoint an investment manager to direct investments, or retain the power to direct investments itself. A named fiduciary that appoints an investment manager or permits a trustee to exercise discretion must periodically evaluate whether such manager

---

[10] 29 U.S.C. § 1103(a), (b)(1).

[11] Id. § 1103(a). Three types of entities may serve as an investment manager to a plan: (1) a registered investment adviser under the Investment Company Act of 1940; (2) a bank, as defined in the Investment Company Act; and (3) an insurance company qualified to provide investment services under the laws of more than one state.

[12] Id. § 1103(a). *See also DOL Letter, supra* note 6 at 392.

[13] *See* 29 U.S.C. § 1102(c)(3), 1103(a). Even the Department of Labor has acknowledged that, if done correctly, a named fiduciary can reserve the right to direct proxy voting. *DOL Letter, supra* note 6, at 392.

[14] 29 U.S.C. § 1102(a).

or trustee is acting in the best interest of the participants and beneficiaries of the plan. Delegation of fiduciary responsibility is itself a fiduciary decision, and a named fiduciary can be liable to the plan if it fails to exercise its judgment prudently, in the sole interest of participants and beneficiaries and in a fashion that diversifies the risk of loss to the plan and that complies with the provisions of the plan. The named fiduciary, therefore, must monitor the activities of any investment manager or trustee and evaluate such service provider's performance. Among the activities a named fiduciary must monitor are decisions as to how securities held under such manager's or trustee's discretion are voted.[15]

The allocation of responsibility between the named fiduciary and an investment manager with respect to voting securities is simple: Only one may have direct responsibility for the matter. ERISA does not permit a named fiduciary to reserve any authority to direct an investment manager with respect to matters delegated to the manager's control.[16] Thus, if the investment manager is given the authority to vote the shares of stock held by a plan, the manager must exercise its discretion to vote such securities, regardless of the issues presented by any vote. If the named fiduciary does not want the investment manager to vote the securities owned by the plan, it must limit its delegation to decisions regarding the acquisition and disposition of such securities and not give the investment manager the authority to vote such securities. By reserving this authority, a named fiduciary can direct the plan's trustee (and not the investment manager) as to how to vote such securities.

Because a named fiduciary can cause a directed trustee to act, a directed trustee is placed in a more precarious situation than an investment manager. Where the named fiduciary has not appointed an investment manager or reserved the authority to direct a trustee as to how securities are to be voted, the trustee must vote the securities in its discretion without regard to the interests of the plan's named fiduciary. A discretionary trustee may not be directed or otherwise influenced by a named fiduciary or any other party in exercising its discretion. In contrast, however, a directed trustee must follow any direction of the named fiduciary, provided that the trustee can assure itself that such directions are in accordance with the provisions of the plan and

---

[15] *See DOL Letter, supra* note 6, at 392.

[16] While a named fiduciary may reserve the right to direct the plan's trustee as to how to act with regard to investment decisions, the discretionary authority delegated to an investment manager may not be so limited. *Compare* 29 U.S.C. § 1103(a)(1) *with* § 1103(a)(2).

ERISA.[17] In following such directions, a directed trustee assumes the risk of incurring fiduciary liability, because it must determine that the directions are proper, generally without any input in the decision-making process. For this reason, the risk to the directed trustee in proxy voting will be examined in more detail.

DIRECTED TRUSTEE

Need to question directions from the named fiduciary. Like a mailman who must deliver mail to a house that has a dog in the yard, a directed trustee confronts an ordinary task that is inherently dangerous. Just as the mailman must choose between completing his "routine" task and risking the painful bite of the family pet, the directed trustee must either reject the direction of the named fiduciary or risk exposure for any liability that might accompany an improper direction from a named fiduciary. Unlike the mailman, however, the trustee does not get to see the dog's teeth (or for that matter, the size of the dog itself). In situations involving the proper voting of securities held by a plan, the directed trustee is likely to have very little input, if any, regarding how the named fiduciary reached its decision with respect to how the securities are to be voted. For example, the trustee will likely not know whether the named fiduciary hired an investment banking firm to assist it in its decision as to the impact of a poison pill on the value of the plan's securities or whether the named fiduciary cut a deal with the chief executive officer of another company to exchange votes on issues of corporate governance. Without such input, the trustee can never conclusively decide whether a named fiduciary's directions are proper and can never be certain that it is free from risk in following such directions.

A directed trustee's problems are further exacerbated by the nature of the trust business. In a situation where the trustee is not being paid to exercise its investment discretion, any number of qualified commercial institutions may be able to provide comparable services. A trustee who demands that a named fiduciary demonstrate the procedures followed in determining how to vote the plan's securities might be abruptly replaced. Thus, the trustee could be required to (1) risk losing its account relationship by pressing for information with respect to a situation where it has no reason to believe that a fiduciary breach has oc-

---

[17] Id. § 1103(a)(1). With respect to the directions of an investment manager, a directed trustee has no duty to inquire as to the validity of such directions and, except to the extent that the trustee may engage in an action that would give rise to co-fiduciary liability, the trustee will not be liable for any actions that are subject to the discretion of an investment manager. 29 U.S.C. § 1105.

curred or (2) conclude that no fiduciary violation has occurred after only the most cursory review.

As noted above, an investment manager (or discretionary trustee) knows whether or not it has control over the decision to vote securities. Of course, the same pressures as to losing an account may be brought on an investment manager as on a directed trustee; however, a manager who attains a return in excess of that delivered by other investment managers will always be given deference. A reasonable executive is not likely to walk away from a superior return that reduces the expense of maintaining the company's pension plan solely because of the manner in which an investment manager votes on a poison pill proposal of another corporation. However, a manager whose performance has been marginal may be adversely affected by noncooperation. Since a fiduciary must act solely in the interest of participants and beneficiaries, a trustee and an investment manager may very well be caught between a rock and a hard place—that is, risk incurring damages for a fiduciary breach or risk losing a valuable account.

Liability for breach. Having determined that a directed trustee may be bitten if the named fiduciary is unleashed and acts improperly, the next part of the analysis is to ascertain how much pain such a bite will cause. Removed from the metaphor, the question is what kind of exposure might befall a directed trustee that follows an improper direction of a named fiduciary with respect to the voting of securities owned by a plan.

No court has yet addressed the question of how a directed trustee is to determine whether the instructions of a named fiduciary are proper. A full review and analysis of each decision would be unduly expensive and often redundant; a directed trustee should not usurp responsibility for the matters reserved by the named fiduciary. On the other hand, a review by the trustee that would determine only whether the instructions are proper on their face may have little value. A cursory review, however, may be a practical necessity. Directed trustees receive frequent directions from a named fiduciary; extensive inquiry into the validity of any such directions, absent an obvious conflict of interest or other extraordinary circumstances, would cause considerable administrative expense. Because of this burden, a strict rule that would require a directed trustee to make a thorough investigation in all cases to confirm whether instructions are proper could effectively amend ERISA to preclude a named fiduciary from giving any directions, whether or not proper. Thus, it is likely that if and when the issue is presented to a court, the competing interests of the named fiduciary and a directed trustee will require that a compromise be achieved.

Whether a particular direction is proper should depend on the facts concerning such direction. Among the factors that a court would likely consider are the probability that a breach of fiduciary responsibility would occur with respect to such direction; the amount of loss, if any, that was or might be sustained by the plan in question; the degree of the trustee's culpability; and the scope of the action involved. Presumably, a directed trustee will (and should) have a higher duty of inquiry where the issue involves an obvious conflict of interest for the named fiduciary (such as any decision affecting the plan sponsor's stock) than in situations where no conflict is apparent (such as the payment of benefits to participants). ERISA's statutory structure suggests that if a directed trustee has taken a direction in good faith without any reason to believe that the named fiduciary is violating its responsibilities under ERISA the trustee's degree of liability should be reasonably limited.

In the context of voting securities held by a plan, the most problematic situation is likely to arise with respect to votes on mergers, recapitalizations, or other similar corporate transactions. In such a case, a decision by shareholders not to approve a merger or recapitalization may have a direct negative impact on the value of the company's securities. Such a vote will affect the continued survival of such company and may increase the outside pressures brought to bear on the named fiduciaries of a company that sponsors a plan that holds the first company's securities. In such instance, if a named fiduciary were to vote for or against a transaction for improper reasons (i.e., to assist friendly management), any loss incurred by the plan may be quantifiable. However, even in such a situation, the liability arising from a breach may be unascertainable because, regardless of whether the named fiduciary acted improperly, such fiduciary's action may not have been determinative of whether the transaction is approved. Shareholders generally may have had the authority to approve or disapprove, as the case may be, a transaction regardless of how the named fiduciary directed the plan's securities to be voted. A violation of fiduciary responsibility in such a context can be said to have no economic impact on the value of the securities, because the majority of other shareholders would have controlled the ultimate decision.

As questions move further from having a direct impact on the value of a plan's securities, the question of what damages will arise from a breach of fiduciary responsibility becomes more attenuated. If a named fiduciary votes in favor of a poison pill defense merely because it prefers to see corporate management protected from raiders, and gives no deference to the interests of participants and beneficiaries, can it be said that such decision will have a real economic effect on the plan? Arguably, such a poison pill will preclude a suitor from offering a premium price for the shares held by the plan, but any damages that are found to have occurred may depend on whether an interested purchaser who is or was willing to pay a premium for the company could be identified and shown to have been deterred by the poison pill.

Thus, even where a named fiduciary has breached its fiduciary responsibility, no direct monetary damages may ensue. The mere fact that no monetary damages arise from a breach does not excuse such breach. In *Leigh & Dusek* v. *Engle,*[18] the fiduciaries of a plan directed the investments of that plan in a fashion that facilitated their takeover of certain corporations. As a result of those investments, the plan was greatly enriched. Nonetheless, the court found that the fiduciaries had violated their duties under ERISA and held those individuals liable for their misconduct.

Nevertheless, the absence of monetary damages should give a directed trustee a substantial degree of comfort. One concern of any commercial institution that serves as a directed trustee is that it is a "deep pocket" in the event of any loss arising with respect to a plan. Where a directed trustee follows the directions of a named fiduciary that are proper on their face, and no monetary loss is incurred by the plan, a directed trustee may take a reasonable business risk that when it acts in good faith it will receive no more than a reprimand in the event that the named fiduciary has breached its fiduciary responsibility with respect to the voting of the plan's securities. When compared to the loss of an account relationship or developing a reputation as an institution that does not cooperate with a plan's sponsor, such reasonable risk will likely be an attractive alternative.

ERISA BY THE NUMBERS

Finally, a named fiduciary should be able to avoid breaching its fiduciary responsibility by paying proper attention to the proper considerations. As *Donovan v. Bierworth*[19] suggests, a named fiduciary that takes into account all of the requisite factors and makes its decision in what it considers to be the best interest of participants and beneficiaries should not be found to have breached its fiduciary duties. Although *Bierworth* involved an egregious breach of fiduciary responsibility by corporate officers of the Grumann Corporation in the context of a takeover bid by LTV Corporation, the Second Circuit implied that, had proper and valid consideration of the issues been given, the named fiduciaries might have at least been able to decide not to tender the plan's shares to the LTV Corporation despite their obvious conflict of

---

[18] Leigh & Dusek v. Engle, 727 F.2d 113 (7th Cir. 1984).

[19] Donavan v. Bierworth, 680 F.2d 263 (2nd Cir. 1984).

interest. Thus, the logic of *Bierworth* should permit a named fiduciary to vote securities held by a plan without incurring liability under ERISA, if such fiduciary assesses the proper factors and creates an adequate record in deciding how it votes such securities.

To that end, it would be useful for such a named fiduciary to have materials that generally support the manner in which such fiduciary directs that the securities are to be voted. For example, if a vote concerned a poison pill, a report from an investment banking firm showing that companies with poison pills have generally performed better than companies that do not have such protection for management would be a significant basis for sustaining a vote in favor of a poison pill proposal. If more than one person is acting as a plan's named fiduciary, a formal meeting of the named fiduciaries should be held to discuss the vote, and the minutes of such meeting should detail the data considered in rendering any decision and the reasons why the vote being directed was in the best interest of the plan participants. Because a directed trustee's liability, if any, would be derivative of that of a named fiduciary, it would be in a directed trustee's interest to note the value of such records to any named fiduciary that is giving it directions and to obtain any such material used by the named fiduciary to help substantiate that the direction is proper.

IS THE VOTE WORTH THE TROUBLE?

All this having been said and done, the final question (perhaps the first?) is whether a named fiduciary should direct the vote on shares held by its plans. A chief executive officer does not want the managers of other companies' plans determining to vote against programs that such officer feels are imperative to the continued operation of his enterprise, but the benefit to be obtained by directing similar votes for his company's plan, when compared to the risks involved, may not justify directing such votes. While the risks are minimal if proper procedures are followed, the gains to be obtained may also be small. Any given plan is likely to hold less than 1 percent of any other company's securities. Thus, to obtain any significant benefit, several plans must choose to vote favorably. Helping another company achieve its goals is not without merit, but the Department of Labor is greatly concerned about this issue and can cause a company that attempts to control the vote of shares held by its plans significant anxiety and unwarranted adverse publicity. Thus, even if such directions do not cause liability, they can still cause trouble. A company that chooses to force a head-on collision with the Department of Labor on this issue best heed the advice of mothers everywhere and be sure its plan is wearing clean underwear.

CONCLUSION

This paper has concluded that a named fiduciary may direct the trustees of its plans as to how to vote the plan's securities. Those trustees have exposure in the event that such directions are not consistent with the duties imposed on such named fiduciary under ERISA, but such risk is likely limited because of the nature of the damages that may be involved. However, the paper questions whether it is advisable for a company to control the vote of such securities, even when it can be done in accordance with the provisions of ERISA, given the significant attention that the company and its plans will likely receive from the concerned administrators at the Department of Labor. From a directed trustee's point of view, not receiving such direction is one less complication it has to address in the ever-changing world of ERISA.

CHAPTER 5

Fiduciary Obligation of the Asset Manager

by
Alfred F. Conard*

INTRODUCTION

There are thousands of words in ERISA, but *voting* is not one of them. In 1974, nobody mentioned it. Twelve years later, when the Federal Employees Retirement System Act was adopted, the authors mentioned voting, but only to say that executives, boards, and employees of the fund should not do it.

Voting was like sex in Victorian society. It happened, but nobody talked about it. Today, everybody is talking about voting, about who should do it, and how they should do it.[1]

THE REASONS FOR CONCERN

There are two main reasons for the eruption of concern about the voting of shares held by pension funds.

---

* Emeritus Professor of Law, University of Michigan.

The author acknowledges the invaluable research assistance of Joseph Coyne and the helpful critiques of Merritt Fox, Tamar Frankel, Robert A. G. Monks, Joel Seligman, and G. Joseph Vining.

[1] The Pension and Welfare Benefits Administration (PWBA) issued its first official statement on the manner of voting in a letter of Alan D. Lebowitz, deputy assistant Secretary of Labor, to Mr. Helmuth Fandl, chairman of the Retirement Board of Avon Products, Inc., Feb. 23, 1988, hereinafter *Avon Products letter,* Pension Plan Guide (CCH) ¶ 23,747, 15 BNA PENS. RPTR. 378 (1988).

The Conflict of Interests

One of these is the emergence of a pervasive conflict between the interests of corporation executives and the interests of investors; Jack Coffee called it "Shareholders versus Managers."[2] The spectacular evidence of this conflict is the series of takeover battles, in which bidders offer shareholders sensational premiums over market price, and target executives exhaust corporation assets in gambits to prevent shareholders from receiving these premiums.[3] Exhibit 1 is a graphic presentation that appeared in the *Journal of Financial Economics* in 1983.[4]

The upper figure shows the positive returns to target shareholders in 211 bids that succeeded, and the lower figure the negative returns in 91 bids that failed, from 1962 to 1976. More detailed figures would only accentuate the difference.[5]

Shareholders in target companies that defeat takeover bids are not the only losers. Bidders' shareholders also lose, as we see in Exhibit 2.[6]

Here we see in the upper figure that shareholders of takeover bidders lost market value in the aggregate, even when bids succeeded, and even more when bids failed.

All these figures are aggregates; they blend cases in which shareholders gained with cases in which they lost. But they offer persuasive evidence that the executives of many target firms are acting against the interests of their shareholders when they resist bids, while executives of many bidders are acting against their shareholders' interest when they launch bids.[7] In too many cases, executives act like medieval

---

[2] Coffee, *Shareholders versus Managers: The Strain in the Corporate Web,* 85 Mich. L. Rev. 1 (1986); *Cf.* J. Brooks, *The Takeover Game* 223–255 (1987).

[3] *See* Grundfest and Black, *Stock Market Profits from Takeover Activity between 1981 and 1986,* SEC News Release, Sept. 28, 1987.

[4] From Asquith, *Merger Bids, Uncertainty, and Stockholder Returns,* 11 J. Fin. Econ. 51, 62 (1983). The diagrams represent average cumulative returns for 196 successful and 89 unsuccessful bidding firms from 60 days before until 60 days after the merger day in the period 1962 to 1976. Asquith uses the term *merger bids* to designate public offers that are generally known in legal literature as *takeover bids.* For a tabulation of results of several studies with similar results, *see* Jensen & Ruback, *The Market for Corporate Control,* 11 J. Fin. Econ. 5 (1983).

[5] *See, e.g.,* Bradley, Desai and Kim, *The Rationale behind Interfirm Tender Offers,* 11 J. Fin. Econ. 183 (1983).

[6] From Asquith, *supra* note 4, at 63. For more recent data to the same effect, *see* Varaiya and Ferris, *Overpaying in Corporate Takeovers: The Winner's Curse,* Financial Analysts J., May–June 1987, p. 64.

[7] For the adverse effect of defenses on target shareholders, *see* Easterbrook and Jarrell, *Do Targets Gain from Defeating Tender Offers?* 59 Nw. U. L. Rev. 277 (1984); Easterbrook and Fischel, *Takeover Bids, Defensive Tactics, and Shareholder Welfare,* 36 Bus. Law. 1 (1981).

EXHIBIT 1 Returns to Target Shareholders

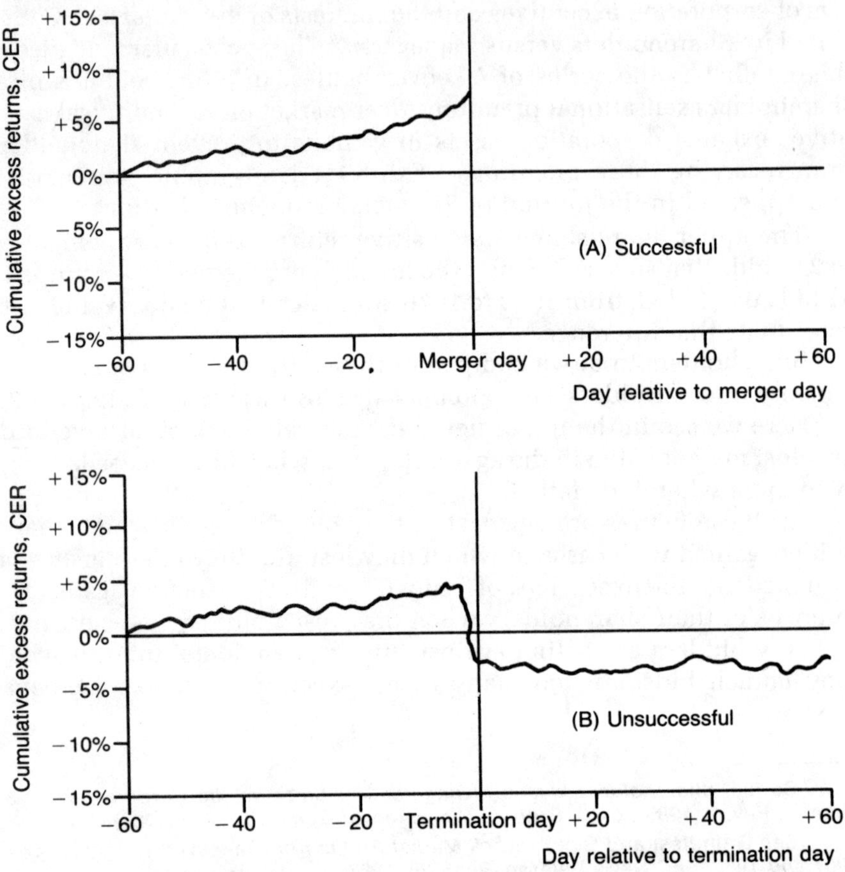

SOURCE: Asquith, *Merger Bids, Uncertainty, and Stockholder Returns,* 11 J. Fin. Econ. 51, 62 (1983).

kings, waging wars to gain territory or to save their thrones without regard to the welfare of their populations.

Takeovers are not the only area in which this conflict emerges; they are just the area in which the conflict is currently most obvious. The conflict exists in other areas, such as executive compensation and dividend distributions. It is a natural result of shareholders' loss of control of corporations through the dispersion of individual shareholders, and the passivity of institutional shareholders.[8] A few years ago, financial

[8] *See* E. Herman, *Corporate Control, Corporate Power* 53–113 (1981); A. Berle and G. Means, *The Modern Corporation and Private Property* (1933).

EXHIBIT 2 Returns to Bidders' Shareholders

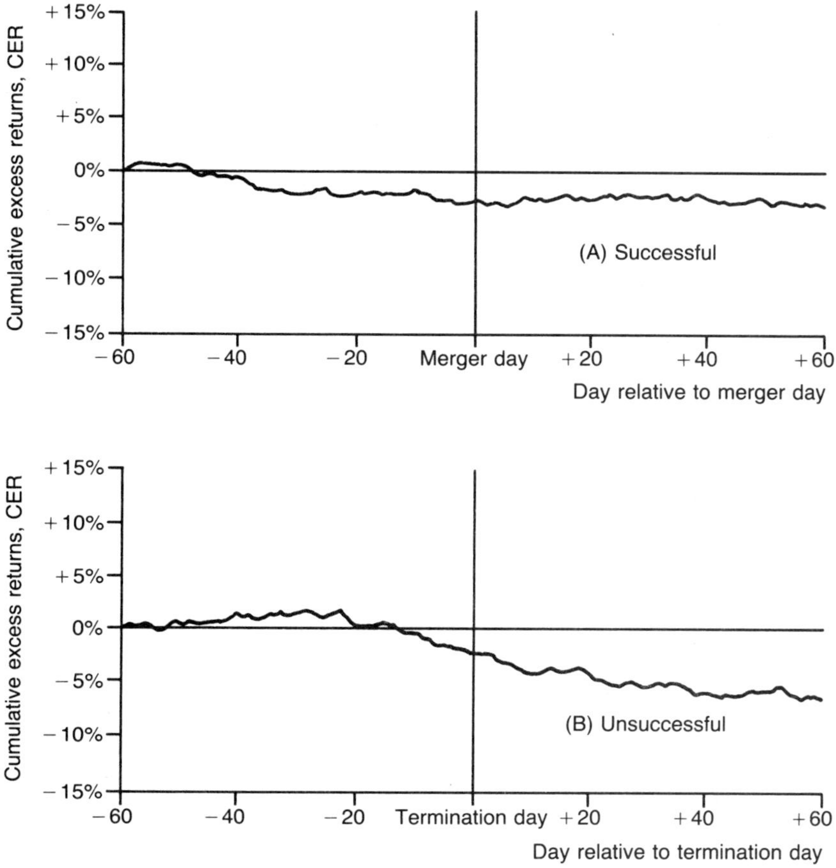

SOURCE: Asquith, *Merger Bids, Uncertainty, and Stockholder Returns,* 11 J. Fin. Econ. 51, 63 (1983).

economists propounded the theory that managerial fidelity was enforced by the "market for control."[9] But a series of successful defenses against takeover bids, with judicial approval, have destroyed any illusion about the efficiency of that market.[10]

[9] *See* Fischel, *The Corporate Governance Movement,* 35 Vand. L. Rev. 1259 (1982); Manne, *Mergers and the Market for Corporate Control,* 73 J. Pol. Econ. 110 (1965).

[10] *See* J. Brooks, *The Takeover Game* 192–203 (1987); Lipton, *Corporate Governance in the Age of Finance Corporatism,* 136 U. PA. L. Rev. 28–35 (1987).

The Power of Funds

The second reason why the fiduciary duty in voting has become critical is the explosion of fund ownership of shares.[11] In nearly half of major firms, more than half the shares are held by pension funds and other institutions. Exhibit 3 is a graphic presentation of the distribution of institutional holdings in a sample of actively traded securities on the New York Stock Exchange in 1987.[12]

Starting at the right hand side of the figure, we see a column representing the firms of which 70 to 80 percent of the shares were held by institutions; there were 7 of these in our sample of 100. Moving to the left, the next column shows the firms of which 60 to 70 percent were held by institutions. These numbered 10 out of 100. The next column, representing firms that were 50 to 60 percent institutionally owned, shows another 21. Putting these groups together, 38 of 100 firms were more than 50 percent owned by institutions. If we add in the next column, we find that 58 out of 100 firms were more than 40 percent owned by institutions.[13]

---

[11] *See* R. Ippolito, *Pensions, Economics and Public Policy* (1986); P. Drucker, *The Unseen Revolution: How Pension Fund Socialism Came to America* (1976); D. Baum and N. Stiles, *The Silent Partners* (1965).

In this paper, I use *funds* as a shorthand for *institutional investors,* and *firms* as a shorthand for *corporations* and *other issuers of shares held in fund portfolios.*

[12] These data were drawn from Moody's *Handbook of Common Stocks,* Winter 1987–88. Most of them represent information as of the end of 1986, or of fiscal 1987. They are based on reports by "institutional investors" to the SEC and to private financial reporting agencies.

[13] These figures are conservative, because they reflect only the institutions that reported their holdings to the SEC or to private financial reporting services. The *NYSE Factbook* reported that in 1980, 35.4 percent of NYSE equities were held by reporting institutions, but that if nonreporting institutions were included, the institutional fraction would probably equal one half of all NYSE equities. *NYSE Factbook,* 1985, p. 55.

The figures represented in the diagram, with additional figures separating firms by size, are shown in the following table.

Percentages of Firm Equity Held by Funds

	Percent of Shares Held by Funds										
Class of Firms	*0 to 10*	*11 to 20*	*21 to 30*	*31 to 40*	*41 to 50*	*51 to 60*	*61 to 70*	*71 to 80*	*81 to 90*	*91 to 100*	*Totals*
All firms	6	5	11	20	20	21	10	7	0	0	100
Firms with assets over one billion	5	2	9	11	18	25	14	16	0	0	100
Firms with assets under one billion	7	7	13	27	21	18	7	0	0	0	100

EXHIBIT 3 Percentages of Firm Equity Held by Funds

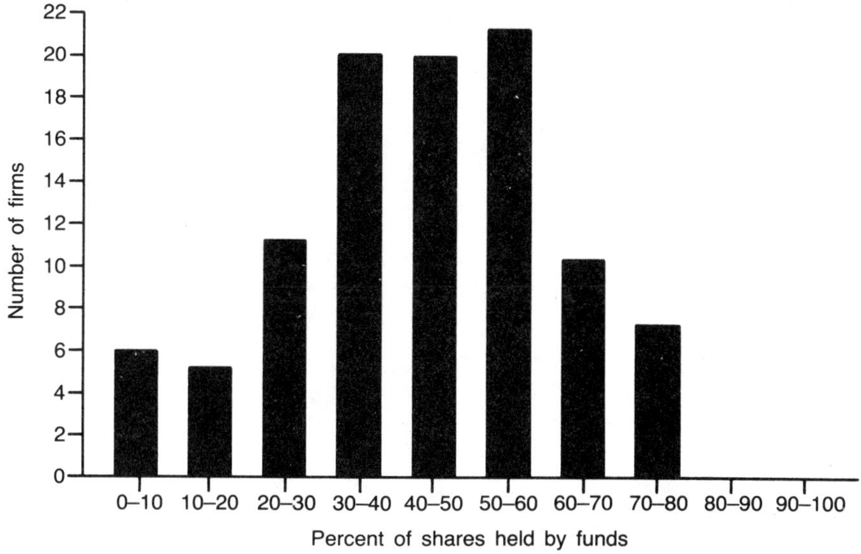

These figures would not be very important if the funds that held these percentages numbered in the tens of thousands, as individual shareholders do. But the number of reporting funds in each firm was generally under 200, and hardly ever over 1,000.

Exhibit 4 shows the number of fund shareholders per firm.[14]

[14] The figures represented in this diagram are the following:

Percentages of Firms with Various Numbers of Fund Shareholders

	Numbers of Fund Shareholders										
Percent of Firms	*0–100*	*101–200*	*201–300*	*301–400*	*401–500*	*501–600*	*601–700*	*701–800*	*801–900*	*901–1000*	*Totals*
All firms in sample	50	23	9	6	3	3	2	2	2	0	100
Firms with majority fund ownership	24	34	13	11	3	5	5	5	0	0	100
Firms with less than majority fund ownership	67	16	6	3	3	2	0	0	3	0	100

EXHIBIT 4 Numbers of Funds Holding Shares

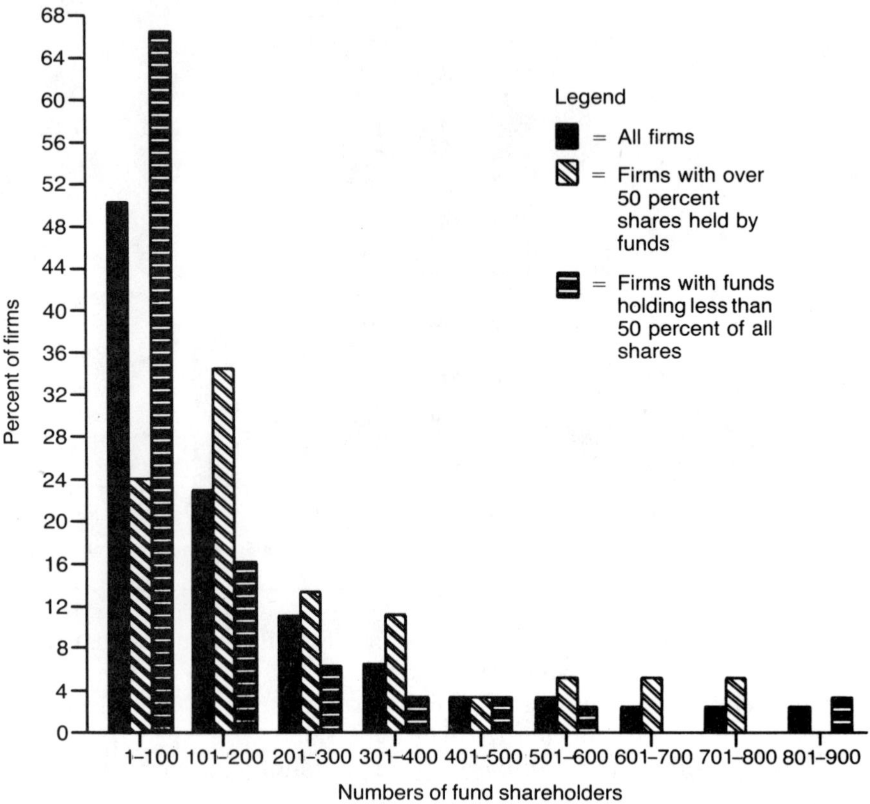

The group of three columns on the far left represents the firms with 100 or fewer fund shareholders. The black column in this group shows the percent of all firms whose reported fund shareholders numbered no more than 100. They comprised 50 percent of the sample.

More significant is the number of funds required to make up a majority of a firm's shares. That is shown by the barred column in each group. The barred column in the first group shows that 24 percent of the firms that were majority owned by funds had no more than 100 fund shareholders.

Moving to the second group of columns, the barred column in this group shows that 34 percent of the majority-owned firms had between 101 and 200 fund shareholders.

Moving to the right, we see smaller numbers of firms in which the numbers of institutional holdings required to form a majority were higher, rising to more than 700. This sample turned up no firm in which more than 800 institutions were required to make up a majority of shares. Even AT&T, which has over two million shares, had only 789 reported institutional shareholders.[15]

These data indicate that the mobilization of voting majorities among funds is no longer beyond the bounds of possibility. If funds would vote together, they could block the adoption of shark repellents in many corporations, and even elect directors. Furthermore, the potential of funds grows year by year, as shown in Exhibit 5.

This diagram shows the growth of fund shareholdings from 1961 to 1986, as reported by the Federal Reserve Board.[16] The top line shows that fund holdings, as a percent of all publicly traded equities, grew three-fold, from about 11 to about 31 percent. The middle line shows that pension funds grew five-fold, from about 4 to about 20 percent of equities. The lowest line is that of public pension funds, which grew 30-fold, from about one sixth of 1 percent to 5 percent. They are likely to grow even further as a consequence of the Federal Employees' Retirement System, which is just getting under way.[17]

The growth of fund shareholdings means not only that funds have power to defend the interests of shareholders against the conflicting interests of executives, but that if they do not, nobody will. In more and more corporations, the *non*institutional shareholders are dwindling to impotent minorities.[18]

THE VOTE OF THE ASSET MANAGER

So much for the voting potential of funds. Now let's look at the asset manager's role in this power structure.

My topic is the asset manager who is not also a trustee. The asset

---

[15] The largest number of reported institutional holders that has come to our attention is 1,028—in Exxon.

[16] Percentages calculated from data in Federal Reserve Board, *Flow of Funds, Financial Assets and Liabilities, Year–End 1963–86* (Sept. 1987), pp. 37–38, and id., *Year–end 1961–84* (Oct. 1985), p. 35. The totals are lower than those reported by *Moody's, supra* note 12, and *NYSE Factbook, supra* note 13, partly because they reflect only holdings reported to the SEC, without additional information gathered by private statistical sources, and partly because they reflect all publicly traded equities, rather than the particularly active ones listed on the New York Stock Exchange or selected by *Moody's Handbook.*

[17] Created by the Federal Employees' Retirement System Act, P.L. 99-335 (1986). The act includes a provision for a "Thrift Savings Fund," to be invested in corporate shares. In the words of a flamboyant journalist, this fund "could be the biggest single pot of savings-plan money the world has even known," Rosenberg, *The New U.S. Pensions Czar,* Inst. Inv., Nov. 1987, p. 128.

[18] *See* Spotts, *Duty of Fiduciary to Vote Stock,* 79 Tr. & Est. 289, 290 (1984).

EXHIBIT 5 Growth of Funds' Equity Holdings, 1961–1986

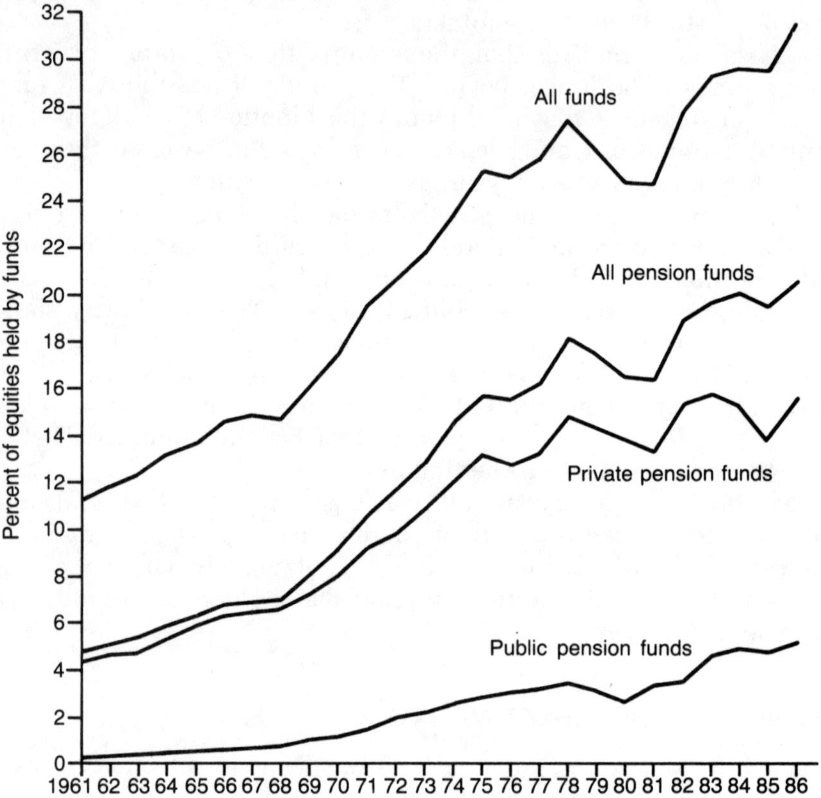

manager who is simultaneously a trustee is the subject of another paper in this symposium.

The first question is whether the asset manager has voting responsibility. The manager's contract of employment should specify whether voting is part of the asset manager's responsibility, or is not.[19] If the agreement allocates voting responsibility to the trustee or to a council, the asset manager is home free. But the prevailing practice seems to be to delegate the responsibility for voting, along with buying and selling, to the asset manager.[20]

---

[19] Authority for the trustee to delegate fiduciary duties, presumably including voting of shares, is granted by ERISA § 403(a), 29 U.S.C. § 1103(a).

[20] *Voting Private Pension Fund Proxies: Some New Evidence and Some Old Questions,* EBRI Issue Brief, No. 70, pp. 1, 17 (Sept. 7, 1988).

EXHIBIT 6 Actors in the Pension Play

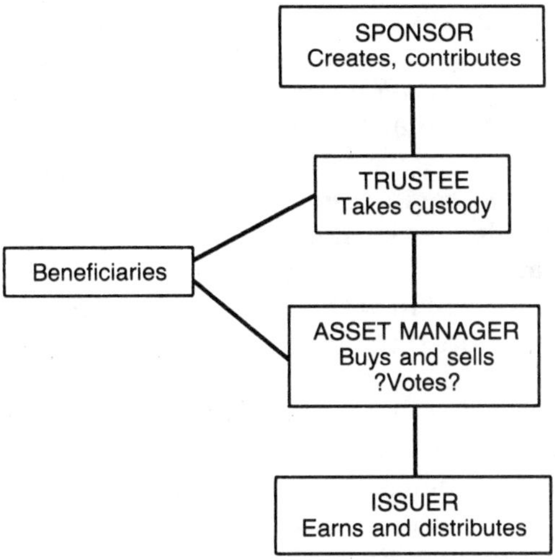

If the asset manager has voting responsibility, it must exercise its own judgment, not the judgment of someone else, even a valued client. That is a matter of trust law,[21] which was recently affirmed in an ERISA setting by the letter of Deputy Assistant Secretary Lebowitz to Avon Products.[22]

The second question is the purpose for which the asset manager should use its voting power. Under ERISA, the answer is categorical. The asset manager should exercise its voting power solely for the financial advantage of beneficiaries.[23] There are important questions about whether a pension plan governed by other laws can or should provide for nonfinancial objectives, but these questions are more appropriate

[21] *Restatement of Trusts* § 171, Comment f; *Scott on Trusts* § 187.3 (4th ed. by W. Fratcher, 1987); Jennings v. Murdock, 220 Kan. 182, 553 P. 2d 846 (1976). In the latter case, the court declared, at 862:

> Voting stock, as we see it, is no different from the purchase or sale of assets, the invasion of principal, or any other aspect of the administration of a trust. Where discretion is vested in a trustee, it is the trustee's discretion that must govern and not that of the beneficiaries.

[22] *Avon Products letter, supra* note 1.

[23] ERISA requires each fiduciary to discharge its duties "for the exclusive purpose of providing benefits to participants and their beneficiaries," and of paying administration expenses (§ 404(a)(1)(A)). *Benefits* are defined in a manner that indicates financial payments (§ 3(22) and (23)).

subjects for consideration by the sponsor or trustee than for the asset manager.[24]

This brings us to the crucial question, which is how funds can use their voting power to advance beneficiaries' interests. If they confine themselves to voting on the proposals that the management puts on the company proxy, they cannot do much. They have no chance to vote on whether the firm of which they are shareholders shall consume its resources to finance takeover bids to acquire other companies, nor on whether it shall consume its resources in resisting a profitable takeover bid from someone else. At most, they can vote on whether to authorize the issuance of additional shares of stock, or other takeover weapons, without any assurance of how the weapons, if authorized, will be used.

Some commentators think that fund shares should be voted against all defensive devices, since these proposals tend to obstruct takeovers, and takeovers are profitable for shareholders, in the aggregate.[25]

This view is too simplistic. It fails to reflect the vast difference between the proper response to a takeover bid and the proper response to a takeover defense. When presented with a takeover bid, an asset manager has little choice. Even if it finds the bid unattractive, it can hardly afford to pass it up. Other asset managers may accept it, leaving the manager who declines it with a tag end of shares that no longer have

---

[24] Because of my time limits, I am bypassing questions about beneficiaries' interests in their own jobs, which may be involved when the pension fund holds shares in the fund's sponsor, or their sympathetic interest in the jobs of employees of other target firms, or in social causes, Ordinarily the plan sponsor is in a better position than the investment manager to ascertain the existence and extent of beneficiaries' nonfinancial interests. I leave the discussion of these questions to other conference participants whose assignments relate to sponsors and trustees.

[25] *See The Department of Labor's Enforcement of the Employee Retirement Security Act* (*ERISA*), A report prepared by the Committee on Oversight and Government Management of the Senate Committee on Governmental Affairs, S. Print 99-144, 99th Cong., 2nd Sess., at 6 (1986), hereinafter *Enforcement Report.* One of the bases of the finding was presumably the testimony of James E. Heard, who said,

> I would reiterate here, Mr. Chairman, something that Dean LeBaron said—there is nothing in academic literature, at least nothing that we're aware of, which indicates that antitakeover charter amendments are beneficial to shareholders.

Department of Labor's Enforcement of the Employee Retirement Income Security Act [*ERISA*], S. Hearing 99–310, June 25–26, 1985, p. 195, hereinafter *Enforcement Hearings.*

See also testimony of Mr. Heard in *Pension Funds in the Capital Markets,* Hearing before the Subcommittee on Telecommunications, Consumer Protection, and Finance, of the House Committee on Energy and Commerce, 99th Cong., 2nd Sess., Serial No. 99–92, at pp. 87–88, hereinafter *Pension Funds;* testimony of Robert A. G. Monks, *Pension Funds* 99–100.

A classic exposition of the view that target firms should be essentially passive in relation to takeover bids is found in Easterbrook and Fischel, *The Proper Role of a Target's Management in Responding to a Tender Offer,* 94 Harv. L. Rev. 161 (1981).

a market.[26] The manager's investment returns suffer in comparison with those of competitors, and it has no opportunity to prove that defeating the takeover bid would have been more profitable.

In voting on takeover defenses, an asset manager's position is more ambivalent. The asset manager who votes for a takeover defense does not forfeit its chance to accept a bid, if one is made. It is free to weigh the possible advantages of providing the target company with takeover defenses. According to one view, target executives need defenses in order to protect shareholders from inadequate bids. This view is taken not only by the retained advocates of target executives,[27] but also by some academics who appear to be approaching the subject more objectively.[28]

The asset manager's dilemma is the difficulty of guessing whether target management will use its defensive devices in order to get better terms for shareholders, procuring a positive return, or will use them to defeat the takeover altogether, with the result of a negative return.

As the asset manager ponders this enigma, it is likely to become aware of some probable biases in the minds of other actors in the pension play.[29] (See Exhibit 7.)

---

[26] *See* Comment, *Making a Prudent Response to a Tender Offer: The Corporation Trustee's Dilemma under ERISA,* 32 AM. U. L. Rev. 839 (1983); *The Duties of Employee Benefit Plan Trustees under ERISA in Hostile Tender Offers,* 82 Colum. L. Rev. 1692 (1982). *Cf. Conflicts of Interest Arising under ERISA's Fiduciary Standards: Can the Trustee Ever Be Prudent, as Long as He Faces Dual Loyalties?* 9 Nova L. J. 413, 435 (1985); *Tender is the Right: Responsibility for Tendering ESOP Shares under ERISA,* 6 VA. Tax Rev. 561 (1987).

[27] *See* Lipton, *Corporate Governance in the Age of Finance Capitalism,* 136 U. PA. L. Rev. 1 (1987).

An officer of Georgeson & Co. (a company well known for its solicitation of proxies) published results of a survey indicating that takeover premiums were higher in cases where poison pill defenses were used than in cases where they were not. Wilcox, *Pills Up Premiums,* Pens. & Inv. Age. April 4, 1988, p. 25, col. 1–3. The author's inference was challenged by an editorial in the same issue, *Poison Pill Evidence Faulty,* p. 13.

[28] *See* Bebchuk, *Toward Undistorted Choice and Equal Treatment in Corporate Takeovers,* 98 Harv. L. Rev. 1695 (1985); Lowenstein, *Pruning Deadwood in Hostile Takeovers: A Proposal for Legislation,* 83 Colum. L. Rev. 249 (1983); Note, *Protecting Shareholders against Partial and Two-Tiered Tender Offers: The Poison Pill Preferred,* 97 Harv. L. Rev. 1964 (1984).

See also testimony of Ian Lanoff in *Enforcement Hearings, supra* note 25, at 27, citing the Grumman takeover defense as one that was beneficial to shareholders.

[29] According to a survey conducted by the Employee Benefit Research Institute, 63.5 percent of investment managers had felt direct or indirect pressure with regard to voting either rarely (37.2 percent), sometimes (24.8 percent), or frequently (3.3 percent). Pressure had never been felt by 33.9 percent of investment managers, while 0.8 percent did not know whether or not they had felt pressure. *EBRI Issue Brief* No. 70, p. 21 (Sept. 1987). The report did not indicate the sources of the pressure.

Among pension plan sponsors, only 23.7 percent reported feeling "financial pressure" at any time, and then only rarely (19.7 percent) or sometimes (4 percent); 75 percent had never felt financial pressure. *EBRI Issue Brief, supra* note 20, p. 14.

EXHIBIT 7 Probable Biases of Actors toward Takeover Defenses

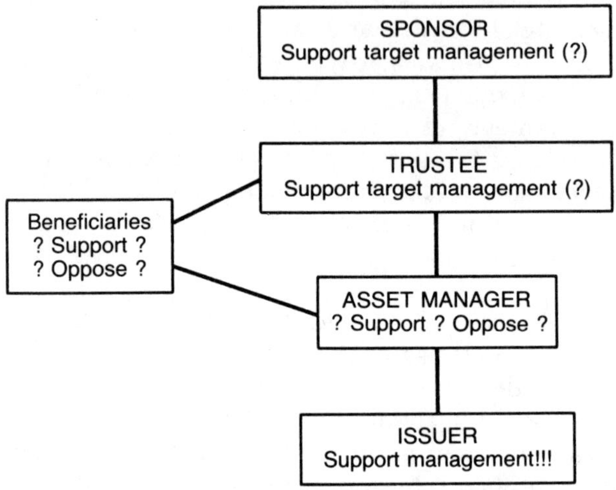

Issuers. One attitude that we can be sure about is the issuer's. Its executives will be sure that their command of takeover defenses is in the best interests of everyone. If an asset manager that holds shares in the issuer is also the manager of a fund sponsored by the issuer, it must support the issuer's management or lose its job in funds that the issuer controls.[30]

Even if the asset manager is not managing any funds for the issuer, it is vulnerable to pressure.[31] The issuer can cut the investment manager's analysts out of the seminars in which its executives make unpublished comments about the issuer's business prospects.[32]

---

[30] According to a recent survey, more than one third of fund sponsors had on some occasion expressed an opinion to their pension fund managers on how shares in the sponsor should be voted by the fund managers. In more than 90 percent of the cases in which opinions were conveyed, the fund managers voted in line with the sponsors' opinions. *See Taking the Offensive,* Inst. Inv., Dec. 1987, p. 101.

There is a considerable line of cases in which federal courts disapproved the actions of ESOP trustees in rejecting tender offers for fund shares, or buying additional shares for the fund, or both, in opposition to a takeover bid. *See* Danaher v. Chicago Pneumatic Tool Co., 635 F. Supp. 246 (S.D. N.Y. 1986); Donovan v. Bierwirth, 538 F. Supp. 463 (E.D. N.Y. 1981), modified, 680 F.2d 263 (2d Cir. 1982), *cert. denied* 459 U.S. 1069 (1982); further proceedings, 754 F.2d 1049 (2d Cir. 1985). These cases dealt with purchases and sales, not voting.

[31] *See* testimony of former OPWB administrators Robert A. G. Monks, Jeffrey N. Clayton, and Ian Lanoff in *Enforcement Hearings, supra* note 25, at 10, 17, 25.

[32] *See* Guyon, *Company Meetings with Analysts Raise Questions about Disclosure,* The Wall St. J., Dec. 17, 1987, p. 23, col. 4–6. This article describes the exclusion of reporters from seminars. If a company can bar reporters, it can also bar disfavored analysts.

Sponsors. Sponsors have no direct interest in how their asset managers vote shares in other companies, but many sponsors' executives harbor a strong bias against takeover bids in general. Some of them think that their funds strike a blow for national prosperity when they thwart a hostile tender offer, even if they sacrifice gains on the shares involved.

Besides, executives stick together.[33]

Whatever their reasons may be, many sponsor executives have put pressure on fund trustees or investment managers to support takeover defenses in other companies.[34] The CEO of a company that had recently defeated a hostile tender offer, and had been sustained by the Delaware Supreme Court, told me, "We tell the managers of all our funds to support management unless we specifically authorize them to do otherwise."

But sponsors do not need to tell their asset managers how they want them to vote. A trustee does not need to assign reasons for switching asset managers, but asset managers can usually tell what the reasons are.

Trustees. Trustees are less likely to have an organizational bias against takeovers, but some of them, especially trust departments of banks, are vulnerable to client pressures in favor of takeover defenses.

Beneficiaries. Beneficiaries of pension funds are seldom consulted, but if they were, most of those who would have any opinions would probably favor takeover defenses. Employees tend to view takeovers as threats to their jobs, although there is no quantitative evidence that the jobs of any but the higher executives are placed in greater peril by a change of ownership.[35]

Asset Managers. As a matter of law, an asset manager should disregard all these opinions and pressures. It should oppose takeover weapons and takeover defenses when it has no assurance about how they will be used, even though it will lose accounts by doing so.[36]

But the juridical risk of liability for supporting the managements of issuers is small in comparison with the risk of losing accounts by op-

---

[33] *See* Cox and Munsinger, *Bias in the Boardroom: Psychological Foundations and Legal Implications of Corporate Cohesion,* 48 L. & Contemp. Probl. 83 (1985); M. Useem, *The Inner Circle* 175–179 (1985).

[34] Rosenberg, *The Proxy Voting Crackdown,* Inst. Inv., April 1988, p. 105.

[35] *See* Grundfest, *Job Loss and Takeovers,* SEC News Release, Mar. 11, 1988; Armstrong, *In Defense of Takeovers,* Inst. Inv., April 1988, p. 29.

[36] *See* NLRB v. Amax Coal Co., 453 U.S. 322, 334 (1981): "The language and legislative history of § 303(a)(5) [of the Labor-Management Relations Act] and ERISA therefore demonstrate that an employee benefit fund trustee is a fiduciary whose duty to the trust beneficiaries must overcome any loyalty to the party that appointed him." *See also* Leigh v. Engle, 727 F.2d 113 (7th Cir. 1984).

posing issuer managements. The Assistant Secretary of Labor for Pension and Welfare Benefits may write admonitory letters, but he cannot himself impose any penalties on the asset manager. In order to evoke sanctions, he must persuade a federal court that the asset manager acted unreasonably in entrusting target executives with defensive weapons.[37] Even when judges think that executives of a target company violated *their* fiduciary duty,[38] they are unlikely to find that the *asset manager* should have foreseen the unfaithful behavior of target executives.[39]

As asset managers ponder the question whether target executives will use defensive weapons well or ill, they can hardly fail to perceive that the risks to themselves of voting to oppose target executives are considerably greater than the risks of voting to support them. As anyone might expect, asset managers resolve these uncertainties in favor of takeover defenses substantially more often than do public pension funds, as shown by Exhibit 8.[40]

This table shows that public pension funds voted *against* a set of takeover defenses in the ratio of 61 to 39, while investment managers voted *in favor* of takeover defenses in the same ratio. The divergence is particularly marked in the first two items, which are most directly related to takeovers. Public pension funds voted against classified boards in the ratio of 90 to 10, while investment managers split 50–50. Proposals to authorize blank preferred stock, which were opposed by

---

[37] The principal civil enforcement provision of ERISA is one that authorizes the Secretary of Labor to proceed in a federal court. ERISA § 502(a). The secretary may assess monetary penalties against a fiduciary that deals with assets in its own interest, but this provision appears to cover financial dealings, rather than voting. ERISA §§ 502(i), 406. *See also* Editorial, *It's Merely a Lot of Noise,* Pens. & Inv. Age, Mar. 7, 1988, p. 10, col. 1.

[38] *See, e.g.,* Norlin Corp. v. Rooney, Pace, Inc., 744 F.2d 255 (2d Cir. 1984); Revlon v. MacAndrews & Forbes Holdings, Inc., 506 A.2d 173 (Del. 1986).

[39] An indulgent attitude toward the business judgment of asset managers is suggested by the tolerant view that judges have displayed toward antitakeover activity by target executives. *See, e.g.,* Moran v. Household International, Inc., 490 A.2d 1059 (Del. 1985); Unocal Corp. v. Mesa Petroleum Co., 493 A.2d 946 (Del Ch. 1985); Ivanhoe Partners v. Newmont Mining Corp., FED. SEC. L. REP. (CCH) 93,552 (Del. 1987); Note, *Share and Share Unlike: Judicial Response to Poison Pill Discrimination among Shareholders of the Same Class,* 33 Wayne L. Rev. 1067 (1987).

[40] The data are taken from Marcil & O'Hara, *Voting by Institutional Investors on Corporate Governance Issues in the 1987 Proxy Season* 38 (IRRC Corporate Governance Service, 1987). The figures shown for investment managers' votes on "Classified board" contain a correction distributed by IRRC after the original printing. The averages were calculated by the author of this paper.

The term *investment manager,* which is used by Marcil & O'Hara, is assumed to refer to the same class of actors characterized in other parts of this paper as *asset managers.*

EXHIBIT 8 Votes on Management Proposals by IRRC Survey Respondents

	Survey Votes			
	Public Pension Funds		*Investment Managers*	
	Pro	*Con*	*Pro*	*Con*
Classified board	10%	90%	50%	50%
Authorize blank preferred	12	88	35	65
Increase blank preferred	53	47	55	45
Increase authorized common	47	53	77	23
Antigreenmail provisions	74	26	87	13
Averages	39%	61%	61%	39%

SOURCE: Marcil & O'Hara, *Voting by Institutional Investors on Corporate Governance Issues in the 1987 Proxy Season* 38 (IRRC Corporate Governance Service, 1987).

majorities of both groups, were opposed by public funds in the ratio of 88 to 12 and by investment managers in the ratio of 65 to 35.

Since plausible arguments can be made for a vote on either side of these proposals, the sources of the divergence are speculative. Surely one factor is the greater ease of voting for management than against it. Another may be that investment managers, being themselves in the private sector, are less suspicious of the motives of executives than are the state employees that manage the public funds. But since a number of investment managers have reported feeling pressure from sponsors and clients, a significant part of the difference is probably attributable to these pressures, rather than to differences in analysts' opinions on the merits.

This state of affairs puts asset managers in an intolerable position. In many instances, they would serve the interest of beneficiaries by voting against management proposals; but if they did, they might impair their access to information, and even lose their accounts to other asset managers that are more compliant.

The result is unfortunate not only for asset managers, but also for the national economy. It means that there is sometimes no cure, short of bankruptcy, for inefficient or self-serving managements. This might be called the acquired immune deficiency syndrome of American business. Fortunately, the disease does not infect all companies, but it may spread if more and more institutional shareholders become paralyzed by the pressures that issuers put on asset managers.

THERAPEUTICS

All of us here share responsibility for this syndrome, and for finding a cure for it.

One suggested solution is to remove voting responsibility from asset managers and allocate it to sponsors.[41] This is no cure. Sponsors are among the sources of bias. Besides, they have neither the data nor the skill to evaluate the management and programs of the firms in which funds are invested.

Advisory councils representing labor, consumers, and others have been suggested.[42] They may have some competence to decide whether the sympathies of beneficiaries are served by opposing investment in South Africa, or by recognizing unions as bargaining agents. But they seldom possess either the data or the expertise to determine whether portfolio companies are managed efficiently and whether a takeover would or would not augment productivity.

The only actors on the scene who are well qualified to vote in the interest of beneficiaries are professional investment managers. But even they cannot do much by voting on the amendments proposed by company executives and the peripheral proposals that shareholders are permitted to insert in the company proxy statement.

The best thing that asset managers could do for beneficiaries would be to unite with other fund managers to elect directors who would see that portfolio firms are operated in the interest of shareholders. That is the statutory model of corporate governance. Exhibit 9 is a schematic presentation of it.

If institutional investors would elect directors who represent shareholders rather than incumbent executives, they would not have to worry about takeover bids and takeover defenses that conflict with shareholder interests. Investor-oriented directors would make sure that these and other activities are conducted in the interest of shareholders, rather than of incumbent executives. Even better, inefficient executives would be removed without the destruction of takeover wars.

Why does it not happen?

There are several obstacles. Some of them are in the institutions' own attitudes; others are in the legal system. (See Exhibit 10.)

---

[41] *Enforcement Report, supra* note 25, at 49–50; Senator William S. Cohen in *Enforcement Hearings, supra* note 25, at 30; testimony of Ian Lanoff in *Enforcement Hearings,* at 34.

[42] Testimony of Tamar Frankel, in *Pension Funds in the Capital Markets,* Hearing before the Subcommittee on Telecommunications, Consumer Products, and Finance of the House Committee on Interstate Commerce, 99th Cong., 2nd Sess., Serial no. 99–92, at 77, hereinafter *Pension Funds.*

EXHIBIT 9 The Statutory Model of Corporate Governance

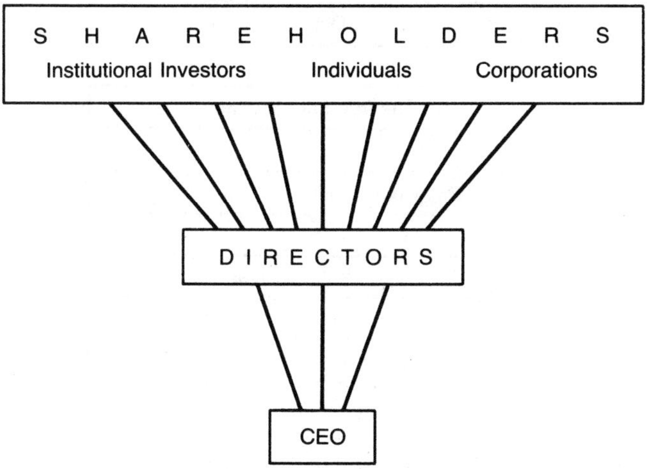

Doubt. The first obstacle to effective exercise of voting power by funds and their asset managers is doubt that it is achievable. Some asset managers think that the dynastic wars of corporate executives are as inevitable as earthquakes and tidal waves. But their doubts might be assuaged if they would take a look at the obstacles and at possible ways around them.

The free rider problem. Another obstacle is the free rider problem. To organize a voting bloc, someone has to take the lead. The manager that initiates action will pay the bill, and the others will get a free ride. For an asset manager that is in price competition with others, this consideration may preclude initiating action. But this deterrent is being overcome by the initiatives of public and nonprofit funds, which asset managers can support without expending their own time and money.

Up to now, the public funds' initiatives have been limited to voting on management and shareholder proposals. But Edward Regan, comptroller of the state of New York, has broken the ice with a proclamation in favor of funds' activism in electing directors.[43] The best hope for

[43] Edward V. Regan, *Pension Funds: New Power, New Responsibility,* The Wall St. J., Nov. 2, 1987, p. 28, col. 4–6; *id., Pension Funds Discover Their Proxies,* The Wall St. J., May 3, 1988, p. 22, col. 3–5. In March of 1988, some institutional investors joined with a takeover bidder in a campaign to place nonmanagement nominees on the board of directors of Gillette Company. Parker, *Gillette Fight to Center on Institutions,* Pens & Inv. Age, April 4, 1988, p. 1, col. 1–2; Ingrassia, *Gillette Holders Vote Today in Fight with Coniston over Four Board Seats,* The Wall St. J., April 21, 1988, p. 20, col. 4–5.

EXHIBIT 10 Obstacles to Independent Voting by Investment Managers

I. Doubt

II. The free rider problem

III. Exposure to pressures of clients

IV. Control liabilities

V. Exclusion from company proxy statement

pension fund beneficiaries is that public funds will initiate nominations and that private fund asset managers will vote with the public funds.

Exposure to pressures. When asset managers start thinking about the possible advantages of joining in the initiatives of the public funds, they think also of the flak that they will get from issuers and sponsors. Asset managers will be hobbled unless they can be insulated from these pressures.

One witness at the Pension Fund Hearings proposed that Congress should prohibit issuers from pressuring fund and investment managers.[44] This would probably not have much effect, because pressure can be exerted so invisibly. If an issuer or sponsor quietly terminates an investment manager's employment, there will be no evidence of crime, but other investment managers will know why it happened.

An alternative solution that was adopted this year in a small number of corporations is a secret ballot, tallied by accountants who will not reveal to issuers the votes of particular shareholders.[45] But not

[44] This suggestion was pointed particularly at pressure from target companies and "raider-investors." Testimony and written statement of Tamar Frankel in *Pension Funds, supra* note 23, at 78, 84.

[45] This proposal was advanced in several firms by New York City Retirement Systems and voluntarily accepted by some. Parker, *Proxy System Is 1988 Target,* Pens. & Inv. Age, Mar. 7, 1988, p. 1, col. 1–2.

Some of the critics of fund voting have urged an opposite solution—that fund votes be publicly disclosed, so that fund constituents will know when fund shares are being voted against beneficiaries' interests. *See* remarks of Senator Cohen and Ian Lanoff in *Enforcement Hearings, supra* note 25, at 33. This proposal seems to assume many issuers will accept this arrangement voluntarily. To be widely adopted, it would have to be imposed by statute or by an addition to the SEC proxy rules.

Control liabilities. A major apprehension that deters asset managers from even contemplating the installation of directors of their choice is the fear of liability for "control." The fear is inspired by cases in which banks have been held liable for coercing companies to pursue policies that prove to be disastrous.[46]

What these cases show is that funds should not tell the executives of portfolio firms how to run their business. They should not even tell directors whom to choose for CEO. That was the mistake made in *Farah Manufacturing*. But these cases pose no threat to shareholders that elect directors, and leave each director free to manage the firm, or oversee its management, "in a manner he reasonably believes to be in the best interest of the corporation."[47]

A more serious peril to activist shareholders emanates, ironically, from a rule of the SEC, which ought to be working for investors, rather than against them. The threat is inherent in the SEC's definition of *control,* which embraces "the possession, direct or indirect, of the power to direct or cause the direction of management and policies of a person, whether through the ownership of voting securities, by contract, or otherwise."[48]

---

that fund constituents are sufficiently sophisticated to know when votes are against their interests. Since I believe that intelligent voting requires an appraisal of the ability and motivation of corporate officers and directors, I suppose that fund constituents would lack the expertise required to detect instances of votes against their interests.

[46] *See,* for example, State Nat. Bank v. Farah Mfg. Co., Inc., 678 S.W.2d 661 (Tex. App. 1984), where a bank was held liable to shareholders for dictating election of a chief executive whose management was detrimental to the company; Hass, *Insights into Lender Liability: An Argument for Treating Controlling Creditors as Controlling Shareholders,* 135 U. PA. L. Rev. 1312 (1987); Lundgren, *Liability of a Creditor in a Control Relation with Its Debtor,* 67 Marq. L. Rev. 523 (1984). Cases are collected and analyzed in *Lender Liability Litigation: Recent Developments* (PLI Course Handbook Series, No. 434, 1987).

[47] The quoted words are from *Model Business Corporations Act* § 8.30(a)(3) (1984). Lundgren, *supra* note 46, summarized the law in these words:

> The courts will sanction specific actions and controls aimed at protecting the obligations due them and will permit limited creditor involvement in the affairs of their debtors. However, if a creditor uses its superior position to supercede [sic] management's control over a wide range of the debtor's affairs and undertakes to direct the method by which its debtor's business will be conducted, it assumes the risk that its conduct will be judicially scrutinized.

[48] Rule 405, 17 CFR § 230.405, under the Securities Act of 1933. The definition is repeated in Rule 12b-2, 17 CFR § 240.12b-2, under the Securities Exchange Act of 1934.

A literal reading of this definition embraces any aggregation of shareholders, institutional or otherwise, that command a majority of votes.[49]

Under other provisions of the Securities Act and the Securities Exchange Act, *controlling persons* are presumed liable for all the securities law transgressions of the corporation that they control.[50] Even more serious, from the viewpoint of an asset manager, they are forbidden to sell their shares without filing a registration statement, or conforming to a limited exemption.[51]

In the face of these perils, asset managers are justifiably reluctant to join in voting blocs to elect directors.[52] If the SEC wants corporations to be governed by their shareholders, as Congress apparently intended when it authorized proxy regulation,[53] it should amend its definition of *control* to exclude direction that is effectuated by electing directors, as the corporation laws provide.[54]

---

[49] *See* Enstam and Kamen, *Control and the Institutional Investor,* 23 Bus. Law. 289 (1968); Sommer, *Who's "in Control"?* 21 Bus. Law. 559 (1966).

[50] Securities Act § 15; Securities Exchange Act § 20(a). The controlling person can rebut the presumption by proving that it had no knowledge of the relevant facts (under the Securities Act), or that it did not directly or indirectly induce the violation (under the Securities Exchange Act).

The broad definition of *control* in Rule 12b-2, *supra* note 48, is not expressly applicable to liabilities other than the duty to register under this section. But there is a dictum that it would be applied "by analogy" to liability under Rule 10b-5. Harriman v. E. I. duPont de Nemours Company, 372 F. Supp. 101, 105 (D. Del. 1974).

[51] The prohibition results from reading Securities Act § 5 in conjunction with § 2(11). *See* United States v. Wolfson, 405 F.2d 779 (2d Cir. 1968), *cert. denied,* 394 U.S. 946 (1969). The exemption provided by Rule 144 (17 CFR 230.144) is limited in amount, and calls for aggregating the holdings of affiliated shareholders, so that members of an affiliated group of funds might be disqualified, even though any one fund would fall within the exempted amount.

A related problem of aggregation under the Investment Company Act is discussed by Kroll, *The "Portfolio Affiliate" Problem,* Third Ann. Inst. Sec. Reg. 261, 267 (1972).

[52] *See* Sommer, *supra* note 49, at 593.

[53] *See House Comm. on Interstate and Foreign Commerce, H. R. Rep. No. 1383, 73rd Cong., 2nd Sess.* (1934), at 13–14; *Senate Comm. on Banking and Commerce, S. Rep. No. 792,* 73rd Cong., 2nd Sess. (1934), at 12; J. I. Case v. Borak, 377 U.S. 426, 431–32 (1964).

[54] In the Investment Company Act of 1940, Congress inserted its own definition of *control,* which excludes control exercised "as a result of an official position with the company." § 2(9), 15 U.S.C. § 80a-2(9). In a similar vein, the definitions of control under the Securities Act and the Securities Exchange Act might be revised to exclude control exercised through the election of directors.

The definitions that the Commission has attached to the Securities Act and Securities Exchange Act reflect the Commission's preoccupation with snaring malefactors—an obsession captured by former Commissioner Roberta Karmel in the captious title of her 1982 publication, *Regulation by Prosecution.* The commission seems to be unconscious of the extent to which its zeal to prosecute conflicts with another of its legislative assignments—to facilitate investors' power over the enterprises in which their funds are invested.

Exclusion from the company proxy statement. Another roadblock in the way of shareholder activism, which the SEC could readily remove, is shareholders' lack of access to the company proxy statement and ballot. The proxy rules require that company proxy statements tell shareholders all about the *management's* nominees for directorships, the *management's* proposals for executive compensation, and the *management's* proposals to amend the charter.[55] But they exclude other shareholders from using the company proxy statement to present competing nominations and arguments *against* management proposals.[56] The practical result is like a Russian election, where the ballot provides an opportunity to vote for the party's candidates and the party's proposals, and citizens do not even hear about other nominees or contrary arguments.[57]

In a ceremonial genuflection to democratic ideas, the SEC lets shareholders insert resolutions of their own in the company proxy statement, but excludes resolutions that relate to election of directors or contain arguments against the proposals of the management—the things that count.[58]

Fund managers and investment managers will never be able to do much for their beneficiaries until Congress or the SEC provides that shareholders have the right to present *their* candidates and *their* arguments in the company proxy statement and the company ballot.[59]

CONCLUSION

Although the most effective way for an asset manager to serve the interests of beneficiaries would be to join with other funds in electing directors who would represent shareholder interests, this path will not be open until some changes are made in the proxy rules.

---

[55] Rule 14a-3, 17 CFR § 240.14a-3, and Schedule 14A, 17 CFR § 210.14a-3 under the Securities Exchange Act of 1934.

[56] Rule 14a-8(c)(8) and (9), 17 CFR § 240.14a-8(c)(8) and (9).

[57] *See* Seligman, *The Securities Exchange Commission and Corporate Democracy,* 3 Dayton U. L. Rev. 1 (1978).

[58] *Supra* note 56.

[59] A proposal to authorize holders of 3 percent or $500,000 worth of shares to nominate directors in the company proxy statement appeared in section 6 of the "Dingell-Markey" bill, H. R. 2172, 100th Cong., 2nd Sess. This bill made no provision for presenting shareholder arguments against management proposals.

In 1980, an SEC Staff Report discussed the possibility of authorizing shareholder nominations of directors in the company proxy statement, but announced no conclusion. *Staff Report on Corporate Accountability* 35–37 (1980), hereinafter *Corporate Accountability,* printed by the Senate Committee on Banking, Housing and Urban Affairs, 96th Cong., 2nd Sess.

See also Seligman, *supra* note 57.

This is not a task for a lone ranger. It will require collective action through an association like the Council of Institutional Investors or the United Shareholders Association. It may be aided by the advice of such dispensers of information as the Investor Responsibility Research Center and the Institutional Shareholders Services.

The interests of asset managers, as well as the interests of their beneficiaries, would be advanced by recapturing control of business enterprises for the contributors of capital. By promoting efficiency, and reducing the ravages of takeover wars, they would confer benefits on the entire spectrum of corporate constituencies.

Today's assemblage of pension fund fiduciaries gives gratifying evidence that leaders of this industry are beginning to think seriously about exercising the power and the responsibility that are theirs under the fundamental assumptions of capitalism. The future of private enterprise depends on the responsible exercise of suffrage by funds and their investment managers.

CHAPTER 6

The Interest of Organized Labor

by
Howard Young, F.S.A.*

INTRODUCTION

At its most recent convention (in October 1987) the AFL-CIO adopted a Policy Resolution regarding "Investment of Union Pension Funds" which includes the following goal:

> Encouraging and assisting collectively bargained pension funds to exercise shareholder rights associated with their stock holdings to advance worker interests in a broad range of areas including collective bargaining, occupational health and safety, plant closings, and in other matters of concern such as support of campaigns to force the government of South Africa to change its policy of apartheid.

That is not a brand new position; it is an elaboration of resolutions that have been adopted for several years. Therefore, this paper will briefly review the history of that position and its impact; then the significance of related developments will be considered. That leads to comments on the outlook for future union activity regarding pension fund proxies and other shareholder rights.

A few caveats must be stated at the outset.

First, "organized labor" does not have a monolithic view of any issue, even when there is an explicit AFL-CIO position as in this case. Since the AFL-CIO has no direct involvement in the pension fund activity of its member unions—nor in their general collective bargain-

* Howard Young, formerly a senior staff member of the UAW, is now a consultant and an adjunct professor at the University of Michigan (Department of Mathematics).

ing—that Policy Resolution is merely a recommendation and guide for the unions.

Second, while most (probably all) of the member unions support the thrust of the Policy Resolution, there are differences of emphasis among them as to the amount of effort that should be put toward that goal, and the activities that would be appropriate. For example, there are different views—among the unions—regarding the desired degree of labor involvement in pension fund administration; of course, managements generally want even less labor involvement than any of the unions.

Furthermore, the structure and other conditions of various unions and industries have produced significantly different pension fund administration arrangements. In particular, unions in multiemployer plans with labor-management trustees start with a strong legal entitlement to shareholder rights, while such entitlements have to be separately bargained for in the plans that have a single employer sponsor.

The final caveat is that I bring informed interpretation of union statements and activities but do not claim to speak for organized labor. I retired from the UAW about a year ago and, thus, no longer am involved in the day-to-day discussions regarding union issues. In addition, my quarter-century at the UAW gave me a perspective somewhat different from other unions, or the consensus view at the AFL-CIO. I did solicit input from various labor sources for this paper and received some but not much. As will be further commented on shortly, the latter seems to reflect the level of activity rather than any unwillingness to share information.

EXPERIENCE OF THE 1980s

The Pension Research Council's 1984 publication on social investing includes a paper by Jack Lyons. He noted that in 1980 the AFL-CIO had decided to "encourage pension fund trustees to exercise shareholder rights associated with the equity stocks held by individual pension funds and to explore the possibility of coordinating the exercise of such rights."

He also discussed a Computer Tracking Project initiated at about that time. Its purpose is to obtain on a reasonably current basis, and make available to unions, information about the stock holdings of approximately 100 large negotiated pension plans.

Even those actions had been preceded by similar policy action at the Industrial Union Department (IUD). Lyons called that "a significant policy change for AFL-CIO industrial unions, which traditionally had negotiated levels of pension benefits but had left the operation and investment of pension funds solely to management."

That was essentially correct, although somewhat of an over-statement. For example, well before 1980 the UAW had made various proposals regarding pension fund investments and related matters. However, those proposals had produced very little by 1980, and Lyons' perspective was that of a multiemployer plan controlled by labor-management trustees.

The sections cited above are only portions of broader pension fund investment policy statements that go beyond the question of shareholder rights. Most unions—whether in single or multiemployer plans—have become increasingly concerned about the utilization of the funds. That is not a topic for this symposium (and, for that reason, this paper will not deal with the question of tender offers or other investment/divestment matters), but it is important to recognize that unions have been more interested in how pension funds are invested than how the shareholder rights are used.

That priority stems at least partly from the perceived limitations of proxy actions: they generally were viewed as symbolic (to jog management or the media) with little hope of winning majority support from the shareholders, or of requiring management compliance even when there is substantial shareholder support. (For example, *The Wall Street Journal* states in its May 4, 1988, edition that a proposal about greenmail, which was approved by a majority of Gillette shareholders despite management opposition, is not binding.)

Furthermore, since unions generally have had little involvement in determining which securities are acquired and held by the pension funds (even allowing for their greater role in multiemployer plans), having a proxy of specific interest is merely fortuitous; access to particular shareholder rights are a by-product of a decision made for separate reasons. That is the motivation for the Computer Tracking Project: it helps unions locate pension funds holding securities of a specific company.

It is relevant to note that, except for ESOPs (and to some extent profit sharing), a pension fund should own relatively few, if any, shares of the sponsoring employer. Thus, the image of employees exercising proxy rights to (for example) defend their jobs against an undesired raider does not fit the typical pension situation.

Those considerations indicate that shareholder rights of a pension plan may be useful to help the employees in that plan, or members of their union or others, or more generally to influence corporate policy, in reverse order of availability of those rights. Therefore, it should not be surprising that interest in proxy power fell below other pressing needs.

That evaluation was further strengthened by the fact that, until recently, hostile shareholder action has been a relatively esoteric subject. The complicated procedures were not familiar to people in the labor movement or their allies. This symposium is itself evidence of the evolving status of the proxy issue. As one further indication, a review of the CCH Pension Plan Guide (which provides very comprehensive coverage of plan mechanics) did not produce any substantive reference to proxy activity prior to the recent DOL-Avon letter.

Unions that got involved in shareholder matters (or attempted to do so) found that the procedures—especially the legal requirements—were very different and much more formal than they usually deal with and were not always well understood by others venturing into this area. Even seemingly simple matters, such as suggesting how the union's own members or its supporters should exercise rights available to them, involve significant legal questions. This is especially true if an effort is made to affect membership on a board of directors, rather than dealing with a shareholder resolution.

The detailed procedural requirements, as well as the opportunity for obstructionist action by corporate management, produces correspondingly high expenses. That would always be an obstacle, or at least a significant deterrent, to much of the union activity in this area (remembering again its apparently limited potential), and was especially so during the lean times of the 1980s.

Those years have been difficult for the labor movement generally and for most unions (as well as for their members); survival, or at least damage control, has often been the main task. Thus, it was hard to justify putting money and staff effort into projects that were seen as having little immediate value.

All of these factors—plus resistance by management of the plan sponsors—help explain why union activity in this area has been less than might have been expected for a long-held explicit goal. However, circumstances have changed.

RELATED DEVELOPMENTS

There are several developments that have further stimulated unions' interests in utilizing the shareholder rights of pension funds: first, the impact of various efforts to impose "social investing" rules on equity holdings; second, union activity known as *coordinated* (or *corporate*) *campaigns;* and third, the general increase in shareholder activity.

As previously noted, proxy activity was earlier perceived as mainly symbolic, with limited real impact on the corporation involved. Similar limitations seemed applicable to efforts to encourage or restrict ownership of a corporation's stock on the basis of "social investment" criteria. That is, many people who favored such actions viewed them primarily as an act of principle. After all, it was reasoned, a corporation is not directly affected by market action in its stock; other investors are the ones really impacted.

However, managements and financial decision makers clearly are very sensitive to pressure in these areas. For example, a Ford Motor Company spokesman is quoted in the June 16, 1987, edition of the *Detroit Free Press* as saying that a major reason Ford decided to shed its South African subsidiary was that "Universities and pension funds are divesting themselves of Ford stock."

Another illustration was the impact of investment restrictions negotiated for the Chrysler-UAW pension fund. The union was authorized to designate a number of companies whose securities were not to be purchased by the fund trustees because of their policies in South Africa. As part of that process, the union established a preliminary list of such companies and contacted the CEO of each one to be sure that the available information about that company was correct. The expectation was that the replies, if any, would involve disputes about facts or interpretations; however, the responses showed deeper concern than that. Companies did not want their stock to be on a proscribed list.

Once again, unions concluded that the nerve link between a corporation's financial sensors and its brain is very reactive. More people came to believe that shareholder actions have greater potential impact than indicated by the vote count involved.

With respect to "coordinated campaigns," a brief explanation will show how they affect the unions' outlook toward pension fund shareholder rights. A coordinated campaign takes an extraordinary labor-management dispute beyond the workplace (e.g., beyond traditional strike action) and attempts to influence management by carrying the issues to their customers, regulators, peers, and others.

For example, if a dispute involves Corporation A and if one of its key decision makers is also a board member of Corporation B, the coordinated campaign may question the suitability of that corporate interrelationship at a Corporation B shareholder meeting or under other circumstances. Hence, the union develops an interest in obtaining Corporation B proxies to reduce the vote for that director and equally (or more) important as entitlement to participate in the shareholder meeting and present the union's arguments.

Similarly, Corporation A proxies can be used for their voting impact and to gain entry to its shareholder meeting for union representatives and supporters to directly engage management in the substantive issues of the dispute. That also gives the union an opportunity to bring its views to the attention of outside directors.

Pension funds are a major, but not the only, source of such proxies.

Individuals and groups have supplied proxies or supported unions at shareholder meetings. Other shareholder rights also can be helpful in a coordinated campaign. In several such efforts, results have gone beyond the raw vote count impact.

Another development stimulating labor's interest in shareholder rights is the generally increased level of shareholder activism. While not all of that has union support, it has improved the climate within which the unions press their own efforts and has facilitated cooperative projects initiated by unions or by others. It also has broadened the knowledge base regarding the procedural aspects of such shareholder activity.

The IUD publication *Labor & Investments* reported in its October 1987 issue that 15 union funds with about $4.2 billion in assets are members of the Council of Institutional Investors. Unions also have supported shareholder proposals made by various groups and have received support of their efforts from various sources.

In short, the perceived and actual environment for union efforts to implement the AFL-CIO Policy Resolution has improved.

PLAN PARTICIPANTS

There is not an explicit labor position on the question of when proxy voting, or other shareholder rights, should be passed through to individual participants. However, it seems clear that the general goal is representation action rather than referendum. That is not meant to imply labor opposition to the legislative requirements (which were expanded by the 1986 Tax Reform Act) for pass-through voting in ESOPs. More likely, unions would favor—or at least not oppose—pass-through voting of the plan sponsor's securities held by any employee benefit fund.

Furthermore, any pass-through should be done by secret ballot. There is no reason why an employer, or union, should know how a participant has voted. In addition, while participants could specify that their shares are not to be voted, that result should not occur simply from inaction. A mechanism is needed to determine votes for the shares of workers who do not respond to the proxy solicitation and for unallocated shares held by the fund. They could be voted in the same proportion as those who do respond, or a specifically designated participant representative (e.g., their union) could determine how to vote those proxies.

Looking beyond the special case of a plan sponsor's own securities, both practical and logical considerations indicate that a representation mechanism is generally preferable.

It is not unusual for a pension fund to own more than 100 different securities, and many large funds own over 1,000 issues. Funds would incur high costs, and participants would be swamped with shareholder literature using a pass-through approach. Also, it is likely that the non-response rate would be very high.

Unless a "one participant-one vote" rule were used, determining the individual voting rights would involve unreasonable administrative requirements. Even the per capita approach would not be simple: for example, would it cover all participants or only those vested (what about graded vesting)?

In any event, workers organize to pool their ability to deal with management, and that concept applies just as well to the shareholder rights in their pension funds. Commentators on corporate democracy have suggested a representation approach to improve the status of small shareholders; following that concept, the union is the logical representative of its members' entitlements in pension funds.

More generally, the relationship between plan participants and beneficiaries in a negotiated plan and their union needs to be emphasized. The plan is not an isolated entity that the participants and beneficiaries look to for future benefits. Rather, delivery of benefit expectations usually is dependent on continuance of the plan and ongoing support of the then active work force to a greater extent than reliance on fund assets.

The union is intimately involved in that ongoing process, and one of its representation functions is to articulate a position for the group. Labor's view is that the distinction, which some people try to draw between a union's representation actions and the interests of plan participants and beneficiaries (the central concern of ERISA), is conceptually incorrect. The union is in the best position to identify and reflect those interests. (Improper actions may occur in any representation structure; that does not deny the general principle of the relationship.)

Of course, there has been some dispute about this issue, and it will not be settled here. Nevertheless, consideration of future developments should not be limited by current requirements or interpretations; efforts can be made to change those if necessary.

FUTURE DEVELOPMENTS

With that setting, here is a forecast for likely union activity regarding pension fund shareholder rights during the next 5 to 10 years.

Unions will make even greater efforts to utilize those rights. However, they are not likely to want—nor should they be obligated—to act on every shareholder issue. They will want to focus their activity, since their resources are limited. Thus, they should be able to leave the proxy exercise to others, but that would be a conscious choice (or at least the forgoing of an available right) rather than a restriction, as at present.

To make that choice, and related decisions, unions will seek more efficient ways to get timely information about the pension fund holdings (e.g., via on-line or other up-to-date computer access) and shareholder issues. They will improve their capability to share that information among unions, as well as with allies, in order to pool their resources. Since, they rarely (if ever) will be aiming for control of the corporations involved, they should be exempt from the restrictions (e.g., solicitation rules) which appropriately apply in other situations.

It cannot be expected that unions will obtain full authority to determine how pension fund proxies will be voted. Presumably there will be some mechanism to consult with the plan sponsor (or in a labor-management forum), and to share authority or otherwise resolve disputes. For example, one proposal is for the union and plan sponsor each to have authority regarding half of the pension fund's votes (similar arrangements have been used in some "voting trusts" with multiple trustees). A subsidiary issue is to develop appropriate procedures when the pension fund covers members of several unions or unorganized employees.

However, unions should have the unilateral right to submit shareholder resolutions. Since that action only raises issues (rather than reaching any conclusion), there should not be objection from the plan sponsor to such union action. Similarly, other rights, such as participation in shareholder meetings, should be available to union designees independently of the plan sponsor's activity.

In that connection, unions can be expected to work with others interested in achieving greater shareholder control of corporations and to press for governance reforms, including more effective ways to nominate and elect directors.

Even those unions that prefer to maintain a distance from the day-to-day specifics of investment decision making are likely to seek a voice (or veto) in the selection of trustees, insurers, investment managers, and similar professionals. That would provide one way of more effectively using union resources. With a cooperative professional, the union can further focus its own direct activity. Thus, in evaluating those professionals, the union will want to be able to consider its general business policies, as well as specific implementation practices with respect to proxies and related matters.

CONCLUSION

Unions have long understood that the interests of their members go beyond the monetary effects of their negotiations; that is just as true for pension matters. Before and after retirement, workers and their families will be impacted by the relationship with their own employer, the economic environment, and the general social conditions. While an adequate pension benefit is the most basic retirement concern, such issues as corporate democracy, healthy competition rather than economic cannibalism, and even such seemingly remote matters as apartheid or nuclear war, will determine the quality of life. Shareholder rights and other aspects of pension funds can be used to help improve that quality of life, without undercutting their fiscal integrity.

CHAPTER 7

The Perspective of Institutional Investors

by

Sarah A. B. Teslik*

CONSTRAINTS ON THE POWER OF INSTITUTIONAL INVESTORS TO INFLUENCE CORPORATE MANAGEMENT

Large public corporations typically give shareholders two means to ensure that management acts in shareholders' interest: the ability to vote and the ability to sell one's shares. The two are by no means of equal value. It is a commonplace observation that the value of a shareholder's right to vote is generally negligible in large, widely held corporations: Small shareholders do not have access to the information needed to resist management effectively; the cost of organizing is great; and the size of the corporation means that the power of even the larger shareholders is limited. Hence, the common conclusion that the only effective shareholder vote is the sale of shares (the "Wall Street walk").

If the sale of shares is indeed the only (or the more) effective means of assuring the working of a key market mechanism (owner control), any change threatening its effectiveness ought to be disturbing. Ironically, such a threat may be developing from a change usually hailed for its shareholder power-enhancing characteristics—the dramatic increase in the institutional ownership of corporate stock.

The rapid growth of institutional investors' holdings is well known, but a few key statistics bear repeating. Assets of the 100 largest institutional investors in the United States exceed $2 trillion. Over 40 percent of all publicly traded stock is institutionally held. These numbers will continue to become even more impressive. The two largest

* Executive Director, Council of Institutional Investors.

California public pension funds, for example, which currently have $45 billion in assets, predict combined assets of $200 billion by century's end. At that point it is projected that over half of all publicly traded stocks will be institutionally held.

The size of these institutional portfolios necessitates large holdings in most major corporations and, for a variety of reasons, makes holdings in small and medium cap stocks less attractive. This, in turn, makes it difficult to take the Wall Street walk. First, the negative effect on share price of large sales makes it difficult for large investors to shift their large holdings profitably. In addition, it is difficult for large funds to find appropriate (e.g., properly diversified by category and risk) places to reinvest money freed up by such sales when their portfolios already contain significant holdings in most market sectors in which they can operate. While this problem may never be too serious for an individual fund's sale of stock in a single company, it will become increasingly difficult for funds to sell all stocks in a certain category (e.g., energy stocks or companies with poison pills). This fact has been documented by responsible studies on the impact of South Africa–related divestment on pension funds. These studies generally conclude that, for precisely the reasons just cited, small funds are much more able than large ones to divest without long-term harm to their performance.

In short, for large portfolios the Wall Street walk will become an increasingly unattractive means of corporate discipline, particularly for matters affecting a number of corporations.

A related development is that the size of institutional portfolios not only makes it more difficult to shift holdings around the market, it also takes away one of the common reasons for doing so. The largest institutional investors are beginning to recognize that, over the long term, it is futile to attempt to beat the market: The size of these funds is such that they mirror and thus in a very real way *are* the market. Recent studies demonstrate that, over time, active management of large portfolios does not, after costs are subtracted, produce above-market returns. Indeed, these studies suggest that over time, managed accounts have underperformed accounts in marketwide index funds. In short, moving in and out of companies in an attempt to beat the market may, over time, be a losing wicket. If you are the market, you cannot beat yourself.

POTENTIAL FOR FOSTERING MARKETWIDE CHANGE

The conclusion to be drawn from all this need not be that managers of large funds should park their billions in index funds and head for the beach (and that corporate management should become even less concerned with shareholder views). In fact, the declining attractiveness of the Wall Street walk and the futility of dabbling too much in company or area-specific matters is being offset by a second development: the rapidly increasing significance of the shareholder vote and its potential for fostering marketwide change.

The first of these two points—the increasing power of the institutional vote—has not been lost on either management or shareholders. Organizations of institutional investors, such as the Council of Institutional Investors (whose membership holds over $175 billion in assets), have been formed to help institutional investors exercise their rapidly developing clout. Responding to this growing institutional clout, business and management groups have formed groups to monitor and oppose actions by institutional investors, backed legislation protecting incumbent management, and provided each other with guidance such as that contained in the recent paper, "Individual Investors: A Counterbalance to Institutional Power," which recommends gimmicks such as lotteries and discounts to attract more individual holders to offset growing institutional power.

The second point, that institutional investors ought to apply their growing voting power to broad-based or marketwide issues (as opposed, for example, to abuses in an individual takeover battle), is being recognized more slowly. This is perhaps due to a belief that proposals to counteract widespread problems necessarily involve ineffectual pie-in-the-sky idealism. But while tackling marketwide issues (on a vote-by-vote basis) may not be easy, it may be the only game worth playing: If you are the market, the only way to improve your returns is to improve market returns generally.

Recognition of this fact is increasing. Groups are beginning to demand, as a starting point, procedural reforms to the voting process. Why, it is being asked, do not all large corporations have a secret ballot system for proxies conducted by an independent entity? Why are the specific results of such votes—which shareholders surely ought to be entitled to know—sometimes kept secret? Should management be allowed to press shareholders concerning which way they will vote? The voting process is, after all, fundamental to corporate democracy.

Equally fundamentally, the adoption of antitakeover charter amendments, poison pills, and voting plans that disenfranchise public stockholders threaten to undermine the value of shareholders' right to vote. This threatens the legitimacy of the entire corporate governance system. It can be argued that some antitakeover measures, such as fair price requirements, benefit shareholders by encouraging would-be acquirers to negotiate directly with management, but measures that make it all but impossible to change control or which deprive shareholders of opportunities to consider transactions that are almost certain to increase stock prices cannot possibly be said to be in shareholders' interests. The fact that poison pills have become almost commonplace should not make them any more comforting to shareholders.

Less fundamentally, why are management compensation packages (that may be key to motivation, performance, and shareholder returns) frequently based on the recommendations of consultants who know their chances of reemployment depend ultimately on management approval? Consultants admit privately that there is a tendency to tie performance-based compensation to tests on which executives already score well rather than to tests that are most apt to measure return to shareholders. Why not have executive compensation consultants hired and assessed by a committee of independent shareholders (perhaps including outside directors) appointed for such a purpose?

Shareholders must not only act to preserve their rightful influence and improve corporate accountability, they must look at the bigger picture to determine how their influence can be properly directed. Groups such as the Council are therefore exploring ways in which they can assist management to improve American corporate competitiveness in the international marketplace. These groups should ask questions such as these: Can shareholders help determine if there are abuses (and if abuses, solutions) in the system that in 1984 required American corporations and their insurers to pay out an amount equal to 1.76 percent of the entire American gross national product in tort claims and associated lawyers' fees? Fear of litigation is widely acknowledged to inhibit R&D in many areas in which American corporations have traditionally done well internationally. Any appropriate improvement would presumably greatly enhance corporate competitiveness.

Concrete proposals like these and related shareholder activism issues are discussed by the Council of Institutional Investors at its various meetings. If these changes are frightening to corporate management, they should not be. No group should be more supportive of corporate America than its owners.

CHAPTER 8

A Public Interest Perspective

by
David M. Walker, CPA*

The issue of corporate governance and the related fiduciary implications are of increasing importance and visibility. Given the size and growth of pension plan portfolios, both individually and collectively, the major shift in the types of proposals being submitted for shareholder votes, the significant potential for conflicting interests, and the related macro-economic implications, it is absolutely essential that plan fiduciaries understand and properly exercise their duties under the Employee Retirement Income Security Act of 1974 (ERISA) with regard to proxy voting. It is equally important for those who recognize the pension plans as powerful shareholders to understand the purpose of these plans and the related obligations and liability of plan fiduciaries under ERISA.

POLICY OBJECTIVES

I would submit that there are at least four public interest considerations relating to the issue of proxy voting of pension plan assets. In my opinion, it is in the public interest that:

---

* Assistant Secretary of Labor.

Note: My comments are not intended to take a position as to whether plans should vote for or against management or how they should vote on any particular proxy issue. ERISA fiduciaries have the responsibility to make individual investment decisions on a case-by-case basis. I also believe it would be inappropriate for government to decide what the right or wrong answer is either directly or on a de facto basis. Rather, my comments are intended to be pro-participant and beneficiary and are designed to contribute to the integrity and security of our voluntary private pension system—on which millions of Americans rely to provide for their economic security in retirement.

1. The integrity, credibility, and security of the private pension system be maintained, and the economic performance of these plans be maximized at reasonable risk and with appropriate diversification.
2. Our free enterprise system include an appropriate degree of corporate accountability to shareholders, including pension plans as major institutional investors.
3. Our proxy voting process be fair, equitable, and credible for all shareholders, including pension plans as major institutional investors.
4. Pension plans that provide participants with direct rather than beneficial investments in the sponsor (e.g., ESOPs, stock bonus, profit sharing, 401(k)), give participants a meaningful opportunity to exercise their rights as shareholders (i.e., "meaningful employee ownership").

Clearly, any actions that serve to undermine the credibility or integrity of the private pension system would be a matter of great public interest. Millions of American workers and retirees rely on the benefits provided by these plans along with their personal savings to supplement social security in order to assure their economic security in retirement. In addition, significant tax preferences are accorded to employee benefit plans. Therefore, any actions that would serve to undermine public confidence would, among other things, provide a possible impetus for additional government regulation or legislation which, if not properly structured, could, among other things, prove detrimental to plan participants and beneficiaries by decreasing the overall level of coverage, benefits, benefit security, or related tax preferences.

Given the many conflicting interests involved in the exercise of corporate governance responsibilities, especially in light of ERISA's specific provision that allows corporate officers to serve also as plan fiduciaries, it is important that all responsible parties comply not only with the letter but also with the spirit of the law. It would be wholly unreasonable, unenforceable, and possibly unconstitutional, not to allow corporate officials to express their opinion with regard to proxy voting issues relating to the companies for which they are responsible. At the same time, any attempts by corporate officials to pressure or improperly direct plan fiduciaries, whether they be corporate employees or external service providers, would clearly be improper and illegal.

It is also critical that pension plans not be viewed as a pawn of corporate management or any other party. In this regard, I believe it is advisable and in the public interest to insulate plan officials from activities designed to present corporate views on proxy voting and tender offer issues. This could be accomplished through establishment of a so-called "Chinese wall" between corporate officials who do not have direct plan responsibilities and those who do.

It is very much in the public interest that the economic value of the assets in private pension plans be maximized, with reasonable risk and appropriate diversification, in order to assure benefit security and maximize the benefits that these plans will provide (i.e., either directly in the case of defined contribution plans or indirectly in the case of defined benefit plans). Any attempt to compromise the economic performance of these plans through the failure or improper discharge of fiduciary responsibilities, including proxy voting, would only serve to adversely affect these vital interests. In addition, any attempts to subordinate the economic interest of the plan to that of corporate management, the union, or unrelated social objectives, would be inappropriate and illegal.

Ironically, many of corporate management's interests with regard to proxy voting of pension plan assets have a "corporate social investing" flavor. For example, some corporate officers argue that plan fiduciaries should be concerned with such factors as job security, including presumably that of top corporate management, and the potential effects of certain issues on local communities. While these are issues of concern when making fiduciary decisions under ERISA, they must be subordinated to the required economic decision. To do otherwise would inappropriately mortgage the retirement income security of plan participants and beneficiaries, open up the door for potential abuse, and, in the case of proxy voting, decrease corporate accountability and long-term economic performance.

Contrary to the views and desires expressed by some corporate executives, the assets in pension plans are not the property of the plan sponsor (e.g., corporation) nor do corporate officials who are plan fiduciaries have unfettered discretion over the disposition of these assets, including the related voting rights. Rather, pension plans are separate legal entities, established for the purpose of providing retirement income security. As such, plan decisions must be based on what is the ultimate economic interest of the trust, which may or may not coincide with that of corporate management. After all, in order for the integrity and credibility of our voluntary private pension system to be maintained, it is essential that pension plans not be viewed as pawns of corporate management or any other party.

Proper accountability mechanisms are an essential element to maximize the success of any enterprise, institution, government, or other entity. Proxy voting represents the conventional tool to assure corporate (both management and board) accountability so that shareholder values will be maximized, not only in the short term, but also over the long term. In fact, pension plans—as long-term investors, separate legal entities, and the largest and fastest growing class of institutional investor—are in a unique position to ensure that corporate America makes the appropriate investments in institutions, ideas, and people necessary to maximize the ultimate economic value of the plan's investment over the long term. This not only would serve to enhance the competitiveness of the enterprise but also would help to maximize America's international competitiveness.

I would also submit that the full and proper exercise of proxy voting rights and responsibilities as an accountability mechanism would also serve to lessen the pressure on more extreme market forces such as hostile takeovers. In my opinion, such hostile takeovers are a symptom and not the disease and, like proxy issues, cannot be universally classified as good or bad. Specifically, the disease is widespread myopia, not only by pension plans and other institutional investors, but also by business, unions, and even government. The proper exercise of proxy voting and other related rights and responsibilities by shareholders in general and pension plans in particular can help to focus the efforts of management, investment managers, and so forth on a more balanced approach that will tend to benefit all of us economically.

FOCI OF DOL EFFORTS

Proxy voting responsibilities relative to pension plans can be placed into two categories of activity:

1. Full and proper discharge of fiduciary responsibilities relating to issues submitted for shareholder approval that will have an impact on the economic value of the stock.
2. Proactive initiatives designed to increase corporate accountability and shareholder involvement.

The Department of Labor's efforts to date have been focused mainly on the first factor. Clearly, any proactive efforts by pension plans should be pursued with caution. They must also be in the interest of plan participants and beneficiaries, cost beneficial, and otherwise consistent with ERISA. In addition, it is important that an appropriate balance be maintained between management's ability to exercise its responsibilities and shareholders' rights for the economic performance of the enterprise to be maximized, not just in the short term but also over the long term. Any attempts on behalf of shareholders to micromanage would likely be counter-productive and normally would not be cost-beneficial in any event.

Proxy voting is not only a responsibility and concern of pension plans, but also of millions of other non-ERISA investors. In addition, many of the conflicting interests are inherent in a proxy voting process and, therefore, also applicable to other investors. While the DOL does not have purview over the generic proxy voting process, it is of interest to the department, given the large and growing size of equity holdings by pension and other employee benefit plans. In my opinion, serious consideration should be given to reforming the generic proxy voting process in order to improve its credibility and integrity in the eyes of the investing public. Specifically, confidential voting until after the results are tabulated, tabulation of proxy votes by parties independent from management, and mandatory disclosure of appropriate information (e.g., votes of institutional and pooled holdings versus individual plan participants) after the proxy votes are tallied deserves serious consideration. These changes would improve the credibility of the current proxy process while lessening the pressure on investment managers and other responsible fiduciaries during the proxy season. In addition, it would put the results of proxy voting "in the sunshine," thereby providing for an efficient means for interested parties to exercise their private rights of action and an appropriate check and balance on any attempt by fiduciaries to improperly discharge their responsibilities. This would be particularly beneficial in cases where the sponsor (e.g., CEO) might attempt to reserve the ability to direct a trustee as to how proxies relating to pension assets should be voted.

Some plans are designed to provide participants with direct rather than beneficial investments in the plan sponsor. In some cases, these arrangements are accorded significant tax benefits above and beyond those attributable to most tax qualified pension plans (i.e., ESOPs). It only seems appropriate as a matter of equity and overall public policy that participants in plans providing for such direct investments should have the right to exercise their ownership interest themselves. That is, they should have the statutory right to pass-through voting on shares allocated to their individual account. This is essential for such participants to have "meaningful employee ownership." In addition, it would seem to be good business, since only through cooperative and meaningful involvement by workers in their enterprise can management expect to maximize productivity and enhance competitiveness.

Many of the same principles that apply to proxy voting also apply to tender offers. Namely, tender offers represent investment decisions and must be made based on what is in the best ultimate economic interest of the plan, recognizing that the plan is a separate legal entity established for the purpose of providing retirement income. Plans are not required to take the "quick buck" (i.e., they are not required to automatically tender if any premium is offered over the prevailing market price) if they feel—based on a thorough, objective, and independent analysis—that the plan will achieve a higher economic value by holding the investment than by tendering and reinvesting the proceeds. At the same time, if they do hold the investment, it becomes even more important that they fully and properly exercise their proxy voting responsibilities in order to maximize the probability that the higher economic value will in fact be achieved.

Finally, I would submit that the full and proper exercise of proxy voting rights and responsibilities by pension plans is especially important since, given the size of their holdings, both individually and collectively, the "Wall Street rule" (i.e., voting with your feet) is no longer practical. In fact, if pension plans voted with their feet on a widespread basis, it would likely only serve to depress stock prices, increase transaction costs, and exacerbate market volatility.

SUMMARY

In summary, while not all takeovers are good, not all proxy issues are either. It is also clear that pension plans will play an ever-increasing role in proxy contests and takeover battles. In this regard, it is important that plan fiduciaries fully understand and properly discharge their responsibilities under ERISA in order for public confidence to be maintained, for regulation to be minimized, and for tax preferences to be maximized. In addition, full and proper exercise of corporate governance responsibilities by pension plans as major institutional investors is also important to maximize economic values, not only in the short term but also over the long term, thereby enhancing our international competitiveness and decreasing the conditions that lead to hostile takeovers.

The department will continue to do its best to serve as an effective watchdog over this important area, but we cannot do it all. We need the help of other interested parties who want to assure that the system works for its intended beneficiaries and that violators are brought to justice. We will also continue to represent the interest of plan participants and beneficiaries in the important corporate governance and takeover areas. After all, it is critical that retirement security of plan participants and beneficiaries not be subordinated to the interest of corporate management or any other parties.

CHAPTER 9

The Conundrum of Fiduciary Investing under ERISA

by
John H. Langbein*

ERISA, the federal regulatory scheme for pension plans, gives pension fiduciaries scant guidance on how to vote plan shares. Nobody doubts that (for ERISA-covered plans) the voting of securities owned by a pension plan is a fiduciary responsibility, hence that the regime of ERISA Title I, Part 4 applies.[1] Yet on a variety of recurrent questions, especially those arising from takeover battles and defenses, fiduciaries have been left in doubt about both what is permitted and what is required. In the present essay I want to put that quandary in a larger setting.

Part of the story is simply that the financial markets have changed in the decade and a half since ERISA. Contested takeovers and social investing were matters of no significance in the early 1970s when ERISA was drafted. The voting of plan-owned securities was hardly on the minds of ERISA's drafters. The proxy rules of the Securities Acts were in force at the time, but shareholder democracy has always been more of a slogan than a reality. ERISA's drafters knew that serious proxy contests occurred infrequently, and that management virtually always won.

More, however, than the changed financial markets is needed to account for the difficulty of making ERISA's fiduciary rules yield work-

---

* Max Pam Professor of American and Foreign Law, University of Chicago Law School.

[1] *Labor Department Letter on Proxy Voting by Plan Fiduciaries*, § I (*The Applicable Provisions of ERISA*), 15 BNA Pension Reporter 391 (1988) [hereafter cited as *Avon Products Letter*].

able precepts for the voting of plan shares. The regulation of voting is not a subject unto itself, rather it is enmeshed in the larger structural disorder of ERISA fiduciary law. In a paper appearing elsewhere, my colleague Daniel Fischel and I have advanced some observations about the failings of ERISA's fiduciary regime.[2] Our basic message is that ERISA fiduciary law misdescribes the economic and juridical reality of pension funds in ways that make it difficult to align the legal rights and duties with the underlying economic interests. The present essay amplifies the view of ERISA fiduciary law set forth in that work.

ERISA imposes a rule of mandatory trusteeship for pension plan assets[3] (apart from assets that take the form of insurance contracts). In support of this trust regime, ERISA fiduciary law transposes from the world of the private gratuitous trust the main principles of trust investment law: the trustee's duty of loyalty to the trust beneficiaries (rendered in ERISA as the *sole benefit/exclusive purpose* rule, often expressed as the *exclusive benefit* rule);[4] the duty of prudence in investing and administering the trust;[5] and the duty to diversify trust investments.[6]

ERISA'S FIDUCIARY MISMATCH

The problem with ERISA fiduciary law, in a nutshell, is that there are huge differences between a private gratuitous trust and a pension plan. The conventional private trust—created, for example, in my will for the support of my widow and children—is a donative transfer. The distinctive logic of a donative transfer is that the benefits are not reciprocal. Unlike a business deal, in a gratuitous transfer only the donees benefit.

A pension plan, by contrast, arises from contract rather than gratuity. Pensions are deferred wages[7] that arise from the employment relationship. Employers are not donors. Employers offer their employees pension plans for reasons of economic advantage, in the competition to attract and retain employees. Employers incur the regulatory and administrative costs of delivering wages in the form of pension benefits because many employees prefer to take a portion of their compensation

[2] Daniel Fischel & John H. Langbein, *ERISA's Fundamental Contradiction: The Exclusive Benefit Rule,* 55 University of Chicago Law Review 1105 (1988).

[3] ERISA § 403(a).

[4] Id. § 404(a)(1)(A).

[5] Id. § 404(a)(1)(B).

[6] Id. § 404(a)(1)(C).

[7] *See* Alicia H. Munnell, *The Economics of Private Pensions* 2–3 (Washington, D.C.: The Brookings Institution, 1982).

in pension benefits. (Employees have a variety of reasons for preferring pensions over cash, especially the advantages of deferred taxation.) The pension plan also enables the employer to facilitate the departure of superannuated employees. A pension plan is, therefore, part of the employer's program of personnel management.

Moreover, when the pension plan takes the characteristic defined benefit form, under which investment risk incides on the employer, the employer has a direct financial interest in the plan. As ERISA § 4044(d) declares, and the asset reversion jurisprudence of the 1980s strongly underscores,[8] the employer who bears the investment risk not only shoulders the risk of disappointing investment performance in the pension fund, the employer also is entitled to reap the gains from favorable investment results, whether by way of reversion, or by reducing the future rate of contribution to the plan.

The basic flaw in ERISA fiduciary law is the fallacy of the transposed category. ERISA borrows its fiduciary rules, especially the exclusive benefit rule (the duty of loyalty) from the sphere of the donative transfer. The settlor of a trust has no continuing interest in the trust that he creates and funds.[9] ERISA's exclusive benefit rule[10] codifies the trust-law duty of loyalty.[11] But unlike the private gratuitous trust, the modern defined benefit plan is a complex multiparty contract for the mutual advantage of employer and employees. ERISA's one-sided fiduciary rules cause trouble because they do not align properly with the multiplicity of the underlying economic interests in the pension fund.

The decision to mold the pension fund into the trust form antedated ERISA. The tax code has long preferred the trust form for pension plans;[12] and the Taft Hartley Act of 1947 mandated the trust for collectively bargained funds, in the hope of distancing pension and welfare benefit money from the dominion of union officers.[13] It is neither new

---

[8] *E.g.*, District 65, United Auto Workers v. Harper & Row, Publishers, Inc., 576 F. Supp. 1468 (S.D.N.Y. 1983).

[9] *The Restatement* (Second) *of Trusts*, § 200 (1959) provides: "No one except a beneficiary . . . can maintain a suit against the trustee to enforce the trust . . . ." Comment (b) explicitly declares that this principle prevents the settlor from enforcing the trust, unless the settlor also has another capacity under the trust, such as the beneficiary of a retained interest.

[10] ERISA § 404(a)(1)(A).

[11] *See* Conference Report on H.R. 2, Pension Reform, 93rd Cong., 2nd Sess., Report No. 93-1280, at 295 (1974) (ERISA Conference Committee).

[12] *See generally* Bruce Wolk, *Discrimination Rules for Qualified Retirement Plans: Good Intentions Confront Economic Reality*, 70 Virginia Law Review 419 (1984).

[13] *Labor-Management Relations* (*Taft-Hartley*) *Act*, § 302(c)(5), 29 U.S.C. § 186(c)(5).

nor wrong to use the trust form to handle relationships that are remote from the prototypical private gratuitous trust.[14] ERISA's mistake was in failing to recognize that the fiduciary rules appropriate to the private gratuitous trust would require modification when transposed to circumstances that lack the character of gratuitous transfer.

RISK IN A DEFINED BENEFIT PLAN

Consider the most celebrated ERISA fiduciary case, *Donovan* v. *Bierwirth*.[15] The trustees of the Grumman Corporation's defined benefit pension plan, who were Grumman officials, used plan assets to fend off a hostile takeover. The bidder offered a large premium over the pre-tender market price for Grumman common stock. Among the steps that the plan trustees took was the use of plan assets to buy Grumman shares at the far-higher post-tender price in order to defeat the offer. When the offer collapsed, the price of the stock returned to the pre-tender-offer price, resulting in an $18 million loss on the newly purchased shares.[16] The Department of Labor, on behalf of the plan participants, sued the trustees for breach of the exclusive benefit rule; and the Second Circuit, in an opinion by Judge Friendly, agreed that the trustees had breached their duty of loyalty to the participants.

The *Bierwirth* case was Alice-in-Wonderland litigation. Because the Grumman plan was an amply funded defined benefit pension plan, the participants in whose supposed interest the lawsuit was brought were not affected by the decrease in the value of the plan assets that the trustees wrought. Investment risk in a defined benefit plan incides on the employer. The people who suffered the loss that the trustees inflicted were the shareholders of Grumman.

Indeed, even if the Grumman pension plan had been underfunded, the participants would have borne little risk. The employer is liable to make up a funding deficiency, which means that the primary risk still incides on the firm's shareholders. In the rare case in which insolvency

---

[14] *E.g.*, the so-called Massachusetts or business trust, *see* George G. Bogert & George T. Bogert, *The Law of Trusts and Trustees* § 247 (rev. 2d ed. 1977).

[15] 680 F.2d 263 (2d Cir. 1982).

[16] The Department of Labor reckoned the loss at around $20 million. Donovan v. Bierwirth, 754 F.2d 1049, 1053 n.4 (2d Cir. 1985). In a separate remedy decision that is wrong for reasons not germane to the present discussion, the trustees were allowed to escape paying the damages resulting from their breach, by crediting to themselves (as a set off) the fruits of the 1980s bull market, which caused the value of the Grumman shares to increase in value after the loss had been inflicted. Ford v. Bierwirth, 636 F. Supp. 540 (E.D.N.Y. 1986).

results in employer default, Title IV of ERISA has arranged that the Pension Benefit Guaranty Corporation (hereafter, PBGC) will stand in for the firm in order to honor the firm's defined benefit pension promises.[17]

The simple truth is that *investment policy is seldom of concern to the participants in a single-employer defined benefit plan.* So long as the plan is significantly overfunded, as many are, the shareholders bear all the risk. In a pension plan such as IBM's, which is overfunded by billions of dollars, the plan participants would be unaffected if the trustees were to go out to Aqueduct tonight and bet a billion on the third nag in the opening race.[18] The victims of the trustees' imprudent investing would be IBM's shareholders. In the private trust, by contrast, every penny of gain or loss is at the beneficiaries' risk. Yet ERISA fiduciary law ignores the shareholders and gives the protections to the plan participants. ERISA woodenly transposes to pension law the fiduciary rule that makes sense for the private trust, even though the allocation of risk in a pension trust is dramatically altered.

ERISA is equally unrealistic in allocating fiduciary responsibilities for an underfunded plan. As mentioned, the employer (meaning the shareholders) remains responsible for funding the shortfall; if the employer defaults, the PBGC must pay the defaulted benefits. When PBGC pays, it has recourse against the employer for the amount paid, up to a large fraction of the employer's net worth,[19] but an employer that defaults on pension promises usually has little net worth. A sick company that pays workers with extravagant pension promises in lieu of cash wages creates contingent liabilities for the PBGC. In such circumstances, the party with the greatest interest in the management of the plan's assets is, therefore, not the participants (whom ERISA fiduciary law needlessly protects), but the PBGC. ERISA allows an employer to create and to enrich past service benefits and to amortize the funding of these benefit promises over a 30-year period, while exposing the PBGC to full liability for the promises after 5 years.[20] The existing scheme

---

[17] ERISA § 4022(a). Section 4022(b)((3) caps the amount of a pension for which PBGC is liable, but the ceiling (which is inflation-indexed) is so high—currently $1,909.09—that PBGC effectively guarantees almost all pension benefits. For current benefit ceilings, see CCH, *Pension Plan Guide* ¶ 15,429B (1988).

[18] "IBM's pension [plan] is so overfunded that benefits are safe regardless of what the assets are invested in, and there is no reason to put limitations on IBM's investment policy for the purposes of benefit safety." Statement of Jeremy Bulow, *The Termination of Overfunded Pension Plans,* in Overfunded Pension Plans, 99th Cong., 1st Sess., Joint Hearing before Select Com. on Aging and Subcom. on Labor Management Relations of the Com. on Education and Labor, H. Rep. 256, 261 (June 12, 1985).

[19] ERISA § 4062.

[20] Id. §§ 302(b), 4022(b).

presents a classic moral hazard problem, encouraging sick companies to take excessive risk in pension affairs. If the coin turns up heads for the firm that makes risky pension promises, the managers and shareholders win. Chrysler in the 1980s has been an example. If the coin comes up tails, as it has for firms like Allis-Chalmers and Wheeling-Pittsburgh Steel, PBGC does a giant share of the losing.

In private trust law, by contrast, only the beneficiaries of the trust fund are at risk from trustee misconduct, which is why trust fiduciary law protects only the beneficiaries. The insight that ERISA's drafters failed to capture in their fiduciary law is that in the ERISA pension trust the nominal trust beneficiaries (that is, the plan participants and their beneficiaries) are seldom at risk; accordingly, the fiduciary rules should have been more concerned to protect the employer's stockholders and the PBGC[21] than the plan participants.

CONFLICTS AMONG PLAN PARTICIPANTS

Not only does ERISA err in neglecting to spell out the employer's and the PBGC's interest in pension investments, ERISA fiduciary law also oversimplifies the category of "participants and beneficiaries" that it purports to protect. The problem is that the interests of the plan participants are sometimes in conflict, a possibility that ERISA does not by terms acknowledge. Thus, the statute does not guide fiduciaries on how to deal with these conflicts when they arise.

The *Bierwirth* case conveniently illustrates this shortcoming of ERISA. The plaintiff in that case, challenging the use of plan assets to resist the takeover of Grumman, was the Secretary of Labor, who purported to act on behalf of the plan participants. Most of the participants, however, supported management's opposition to the tender offer.[22] Most active Grumman employees feared that the takeover and merger might lead to reduced employment. They were willing to trade retirement security for employment security (especially since, as al-

---

[21] ERISA should be revised in order to limit the creation of unfunded past service credits, which means, inter alia, eliminating the spread between the current five-year phase-in period for the PBGC guarantee and the 30-year amortization period for funding. PBGC should have the ability to restrict corporate spending, dividends, and plan investments when severe underfunding puts the PBGC at serious risk. See D. Ezra, *The Struggle for Pension Fund Wealth* 76 (Toronto 1983): "As an alternative to a cumbersome scheme of plan termination insurance . . . , it is worth considering whether the problem is not better addressed by insisting on full disclosure, very rapid catch-up funding for the few potential weaklings in the system, and not permitting them to make retroactive benefit increases until the newly created obligations are funded equally rapidly."

[22] Donovan v. Bierwirth, 680 F.2d 263, 267 (2d Cir. 1982).

ready explained, the shareholders rather than the participants bore the main cost of management's gambit). But some participants could not have benefited from protecting Grumman jobs—for example, those who were already retired; those (typically senior employees) whose employment was more secure; and the beneficiaries of deceased former employees. They had interests contrary to those of many active employees.

This conflict among classes of participants is especially prominent in social investing schemes, for example, the one in *Brock* v. *Walton*.[23] A union-dominated multiemployer plan undertook to subsidize jobs for union members in the construction trades by making below-market mortgage loans. This was a scheme that transferred pension wealth away from retirees and senior workers to the marginal workers whose employment prospects the extra construction activity would enhance. Despite a challenge from the Department of Labor, the courts approved the loans.

The unfortunate outcome in *Brock* v. *Walton* was exceptional. One of ERISA's clear triumphs in the field of fiduciary law has been to restrain social investing pressures. Most of the social investing activity has occurred in ERISA-exempt settings, that is, in state and local plans and in nonpension funds such as university and church endowments. I have elsewhere said a good deal about why most social investing schemes offend conventional fiduciary principles, both under ERISA and under the common law of trusts.[24] My present point is not to cover that ground again, but to observe that in social investing as elsewhere, ERISA breeds trouble by neglecting to identify all the relevant interests. The court that overruled the Department of Labor and allowed the social investing scheme in *Brock* v. *Walton* would have had a much harder time reaching that mistaken result if it had been required to analyze the scheme for what it was—a wealth transfer from retirees and senior workers to younger workers. If the court had understood the scheme in those terms, it could scarcely have reconciled the trustees' behavior with their duty of loyalty under ERISA's exclusive benefit rule.

---

[23] Donovan v. Walton, 609 F. Supp. 1221 (S.D. Fla. 1985), *aff'd per curiam sub nom.* Brock v. Walton, 794 F.2d 586 (11th Cir. 1986), *rehearing denied without opinion,* 802 F.2d 1399 (11th Cir. 1986).

[24] John H. Langbein, *Social Investing of Pension Funds and University Endowments: Unprincipled, Futile and Illegal,* in Disinvestment: Is It Legal? Is It Moral? Is It Productive? 1–28 (Washington: National Legal Center for the Public Interest, 1985).

FIDUCIARY VOTING

In his valuable contribution to this symposium volume, Alfred Conard presents exceptionally interesting data about the spinelessness that ERISA fiduciaries have exhibited in voting on takeover defenses. His sample shows that fiduciaries managing ERISA-exempt pension funds (that is, public employee funds) "voted *against* a set of takeover defenses in the ratio of 61 to 39, while [ERISA-covered] investment managers voted *in favor* of takeover defenses in the same ratio."[25] Conard remarks that "a number of investment managers [for ERISA-covered private plans] have reported feeling pressure from sponsors and clients" and fear "los[ing] their accounts to other asset managers that are more compliant."[26]

We see, therefore, that ERISA-exempt fiduciaries are much more courageous in using their voting powers to resist value-impairing antitakeover measures than ERISA-covered fiduciaries. Notice the striking contrast with fiduciary behavior on social investing: ERISA-covered fiduciaries have been more resistant than ERISA-exempt fiduciaries to social investing pressures. ERISA-exempt fiduciaries of public plans have suffered both from political exposure and from the want of doctrinal reinforcement comparable to ERISA's exclusive benefit rule. Why, then, do ERISA-covered fiduciaries appear to be less well insulated than ERISA-exempt fiduciaries when it comes to voting plan shares against antitakeover measures?

ERISA fiduciary law has worked smoothly to restrain social investing in most cases because the interest of the plan participants aligns well with the interest of the plan sponsor. Consider the current pressures for avoiding the shares of companies that do business in South Africa. Such an investment strategy risks a suboptimal return: It inflicts the transaction costs of reforming the portfolio; and depending on the rigor with which the forbidden group of securities is defined, it impairs diversification by limiting the universe of investment opportunities. In pure doctrinal terms, ERISA's exclusive benefit rule requires the fiduciaries to prefer the interest of plan participants, to whom the fiduciaries owe their duty of loyalty, over the interest of nonparticipants such as the South African workers who are meant to be benefited by having the pension fund accept submarket returns on plan investments. But the plan sponsor, the employer, has an independent ground for resisting such investment practices. Because the investment risk in a defined

[25] See Chapter 5.

[26] Id.

benefit plan incides on the employer, the employer would bear the costs of the lower investment return that the social investing scheme entails. Thus, the typical social investing campaign presents a situation in which the employer's interest coincides with the interest of the plan participants, and ERISA's exclusive benefit rule law works smoothly enough.

In the matter of takeover defenses, however, the interests diverge. There is always a potential conflict of interest between the employing firm's shareholders and its managers. Takeovers threaten managers, not shareholders. The market for corporate control invites contests about who can manage corporate assets better, and unsuccessful managers often lose their jobs. Managers are hostile to takeover activity. ERISA's exclusive benefit rule neglects to address this problem, because—as already remarked in connection with the *Bierwirth* case—the ERISA rule is preoccupied with protecting the people who seldom need protection, the plan participants.

As between the interests of managers and shareholders, ERISA-covered fiduciaries pander to management inclination in the voting of plan shares. That is the lesson of Conard's data. This phenomenon occurs notwithstanding that—as the Department of Labor's *Avon Products Letter* underscores[27]—ERISA's fiduciary rules should insulate the fiduciary from plan sponsor interference in voting.

The explanation for this puzzle implicates a remarkable feature of ERISA's fiduciary law, the permission for plan sponsors to install nonneutral fiduciaries. Section 408(c)(3) authorizes a fiduciary to "serv[e] as a fiduciary in addition to being an officer, employee, agent, or other representative of a party in interest." Section 3(14) defines party in interest to include the employer. Thus, ERISA allows corporate officers like Mr. Bierwirth and his colleagues at Grumman to serve as plan fiduciaries. Without the immunity of section 408(c)(3), these nonneutral fiduciaries would violate ERISA's prohibited transaction and exclusive benefit standards. Section 408(c)(3) is one of those places (like the authorization for asset reversion in section 4044(d)) in which ERISA recognizes the employer's interest in pension and welfare benefit plans. The assumption is that employers will be more likely to institute plans if employer personnel administer them. Yet the resulting conflict of interest can be very serious; it lies at the root of the dispute, now before the Supreme Court, about what standard of deference courts should give to the decision making of a nonneutral fiduciary.[28]

---

[27] *Avon Products Letter, supra* note 1, 15 BNA Pension Reporter at 392, text at notes 1–3.

[28] Bruch v. Firestone Tire & Rubber Co., 828 F.2d 134 (3rd Cir. 1987), *cert. granted sub nom.* Firestone Tire & Rubber Co. v. Bruch, 108 S. Ct. 1288 (1988).

Even when the plan sponsor declines to avail itself of its section 408(c)(3) power to make use of an interested fiduciary—even when, that is, the sponsor selects nominally neutral outside investment managers or other fiduciaries—the dice are loaded in the contest between shareholders and managers. The shareholders own the firm, but the firm's managers pick the "independent" investment managers and fiduciaries. An investment manager who follows a policy of maximizing shareholder value by vigorously voting plan shares to oppose anti-takeover measures is pursuing a course that is unpopular with the corporate officers who select investment managers. And thus Conard's observation that "a number of investment managers have reported feeling pressure from sponsors and clients" and fear "los[ing] their accounts to other asset managers that are more compliant."[29]

The Department of Labor's *Avon Products Letter*, while doctrinally sound, is essentially futile. Because it cannot reach the embedded conflict of interest that is the source of the problem, it is left to incant the old nostrums of CYA, paper-trail fiduciary practice. Appearances must be respected. Employers must go through the motions of respecting fiduciary independence, providing written guidelines, monitoring compliance, making sure that proper records of voting activity are kept, and the like.[30] Doubtless, a few bumblers will handle their proxy manipulations so clumsily as to run afoul of these standards. But in the main, this stuff is window dressing that only conceals the incentives that lead to fiduciary subservience. There is no reason to think that Conard's data, which predates the *Avon Products Letter*, will look much different in the future. Money managers know who picks money managers.

CONCLUSION

ERISA fiduciary law, especially the exclusive benefit rule, is incoherent as applied to investment matters, especially takeover contests and proxy issues. ERISA overprotects plan participants, who are ordinarily at little or no risk. ERISA is insensitive to the shareholder-versus-management conflicts that arise frequently and to the participant-versus-participant conflicts that can also arise in investment matters. ERISA seriously underprotects the shareholders of plan sponsors and the PBGC, the parties on whom the real risks of unsound investment practices mostly incide.

---

[29] *Supra* note 25.

[30] *Avon Products Letter, supra* note 1, 15 BNA Pension Reporter, at 392, penultimate.

APPENDIX A

United Shareholders Association Speech February 17, 1988

by

David M. Walker, CPA
Assistant Secretary of Labor

I. Corporate governance and proxy voting matters—Matter of growing importance and visibility in general and for ERISA plans for several reasons.

A. Overview/background

1. Increasing size of institutional holdings of which pension plans represent the largest single and fastest growing category of institutional investor, (i.e., pension plans already own approximately 30 percent of all corporate equity, 50 percent of NYSE, and over 65 percent of many S&P 500 firms, and by the year 2000, pension plans may own approximately 50 percent of all corporate equity).
2. Given the size of pension portfolios both individually and collectively, the "Wall Street Rule" would not seem to be a viable means for pension plans to maximize their ultimate economic value. In fact, if pension plans voted with their feet on a widespread basis, it would only serve to depress stock prices, increase transaction costs, and exacerbate market volatility. In addition, given their size, pension plans are now finding they are major players in proxy voting contests and takeover battles.
3. With regard to proxy voting, there has been a major shift in the type of proposals being introduced for shareholder votes. Many of which clearly may have an effect on the economic value of the stock no matter how they are packaged (e.g., poison pills, staggered boards, and shareholder rights plans).

4. Proxy voting on issues that can affect the economic value of the stock represents the primary conventional tool for shareholders in their efforts to assure corporate accountability (management and otherwise) and to maximize the value of their existing holdings. This is especially important for pension plans since plan fiduciaries are obligated to, among other things, seek to maximize the ultimate economic value of the plan's holdings consistent with a given level of risk and ERISA's other provisions.
5. As a result of and in view of the increasing importance and changing nature of proxy votes and the rapid growth of private pension plan holdings in corporate equities, it is absolutely essential that plan fiduciaries understand and exercise their fiduciary duties under ERISA with regard to proxy voting. It is also essential that others who recognize that pension plans are powerful shareholders understand the purpose of these plans and the obligations of plan fiduciaries under ERISA.

B. General principles

1. Voting rights have economic value and must be treated accordingly. (Market places a value via different dividend rates or other preferences.)
2. Proxy votes that can affect the economic value of plan investments unquestionably involve the exercise of fiduciary responsibility. As a result, a fiduciary who manages a portfolio has a duty to evaluate issues that can have an impact on the economic value of the stock in the portfolio and to vote on those issues. These votes must be prudent and consistent with the fiduciary standards of ERISA (solely in the interest of plan participants and their beneficiaries, and for the exclusive purpose of paying benefits and reasonable administrative expenses). In this regard, it is important to emphasize that pension plans are separate legal entities that are designed to provide retirement income. As such, the assets in any ongoing pension plan belong to the trust and must be managed for its benefit, which may or may not coincide with that of corporate management. Fiduciaries must keep this purpose in the forefront of their mind and must not allow other factors to override or undercut the required economic decision (e.g., job security for top management or others). Why? Because pension plans are not and must not be a tool of corporate management or any other party.

3. Shares should be voted based on a careful analysis of the impact of the vote on the ultimate economic value of the plans' investment (the stock) during the period in which the plan intends to hold the investment. This same principle also applies to tender offers, which I will speak to a little later.
4. Blindly voting (with management or otherwise) on matters that have an effect on the economic value of the stock is imprudent and may result in a violation of ERISA's fiduciary standards (the exclusive purpose and solely in interest rules). This does not mean fiduciaries must vote against management. Rather, they must decide how to vote based on a careful analysis of the impact on the vote on the ultimate value of the plan's investment.
5. Given the possible conflicts of interest and potential for abuse, managers and trustees should have documented guidelines concerning the voting of shares. In addition, votes affecting the value of a stock must be documented along with the reasons for the vote.
6. The fiduciary (e.g., investment manager, trustee, or other fiduciary) must not vote with an eye toward its own business or private interests, rather than the interests of the plan. Doing so represents a clear violation of ERISA's exclusive purpose rule.
7. In summary, when dealing in matters relating in corporate governance, fiduciaries must assure that their actions are prudent and consistent with the exclusive purpose and solely in interest rules of ERISA. As such, fiduciary decisions must be based on what is in the ultimate economic interest of the plan, viewing the plan as a separate legal entity designed to provide retirement income and security and not other factors no matter how important or worthy (e.g., the interests of corporate management, general job security considerations). This means that, among other things, all fiduciary decisions must be based on maximizing the ultimate economic value of the plan's investment (with reasonable risk and appropriate diversification) since it is this economic value that plan participants rely on as a means of assuring their retirement income security. Any other factors must be incidental to the economic decision. This is a fundamental premise under ERISA, which we have consistently applied to any so-called social investing considerations whether they are

advocated by organized labor or, as in the case of most corporate governance issues, corporate management.

C. Additional ERISA issues relating to proxy voting

1. The Department is aware of interest by certain parties (e.g., corporate management) to direct their investment managers as to how to vote on certain issues. It should be noted, however, that there are no provisions in ERISA for direction of investment managers (since they cannot function as trustees in managing the assets as to which they are investment managers under Sec. 3(38) of ERISA). Therefore, any directions given to investment managers are legally ineffective under ERISA and investment managers should resist any such attempts. Where an investment manager or trustee accedes to an improper direction, then both it and the party directing it will be liable for any adverse effect on the plan's investment resulting from the improper direction.
2. While ERISA does provide for the direction of trustees, they can only take any such directions from persons provided for in the plan document and any such directions cannot be inconsistent with Title I or Title IV of ERISA (e.g., not in the ultimate economic interest of the plan). If the direction is not from the designated person or if it contravenes the provisions of either of these titles, then the trustee must ignore it. This does not mean that management is precluded from expressing its opinion on an issue; after all, freedom of speech is protected under the first amendment to the Constitution. At the same time, any attempts to pressure or direct an investment manager are clearly improper.
3. The Department has also been aware of attempts by named fiduciaries to appoint an investment manager to manage plan assets while reserving to the plan trustees the votes appurtenant to the plan's stockholding and reserved to itself the authority to direct the plan trustee as to certain voting rights. After considerable legal review and analysis, the Department has concluded that while this can be troubling from a policy perspective, it is not a per se violation of ERISA, nor does it cause the named fiduciary to lose its insulation from the individual investment decisions of the investment manager. At the same time, the plan document must clearly provide for this separation of responsibilities and the party to which the

proxy voting obligation is reserved. In addition, a violation of ERISA could occur in the discharge of those responsibilities if the fiduciary's actions are inconsistent with ERISA, including the principles noted in this speech.

4. Specifically, when dealing in matters relating in corporate governance, all responsible fiduciaries must assure that their actions are consistent with the exclusive purpose and solely in interest rules of ERISA. As such, decisions must be based on what is in the best ultimate interest of the plan, viewing the plan as a separate legal entity established for the purpose of providing retirement income. This means that, among other things, all fiduciary decisions must be based on maximizing the ultimate economic value of the plan's investment (with reasonable risk and appropriate diversification) since it is this economic value that plan participants rely on as a means of assuring their retirement income security. Any other factors must be incidental to this decision. It is also clear that the plan's ultimate interest may or may not coincide with that of corporate management.

II. Overview of takeovers from an ERISA perspective

A. As previously noted, given the size and growth of pension plan holdings, whether they want to be or not, pension plans are major players in corporate takeover battles, both directly (i.e., as institutional investors) and indirectly (i.e., pension plans as a potential cause of takeovers and the potential effects of a takeover on a pension plan).

B. With regard to the direct investment implications of takeovers on pension plans, the decision whether to tender or not is an investment decision that must be made by the responsible fiduciary, normally the investment manager. This decision, as in the case of proxy voting, must be made based on what is in the best ultimate economic interest of the plan, viewing the plan as a separate legal entity established for the purpose of providing retirement income and not other objectives no matter how important or worthy (e.g., job security of management or other plan participants).

C. Pension plans are not required to take the "quick buck" if they feel that the plan—based on a reasoned, objective, and independent analysis—will achieve a higher economic value by holding their shares.

D. In fact, since pension plans are long-term investors and given the size of their holdings, they are in a unique position to assure that American corporations (i.e., through management and board accountability) make the necessary investments in institutions (e.g., VC), ideas (e.g., R&D), and people (e.g., training, productivity incentives) that are necessary to maximize shareholder values consistent with acceptable risk both currently and over the long term. After all, the evidence shows that appropriate investments in R&D actually serve to enhance shareholder values despite the assertions by some to the contrary. An important by-product of these investments is enhanced competitiveness for the corporation both domestically and internationally, which is critical given our global economy. Applied on a larger scale, it means enhanced American competitiveness that will allow us to maintain and improve our status as the number one economic power on earth.

E. With regard to the indirect effects of takeovers on pension plans, these generally fall into two categories: namely, pre- and posttakeover activities by the plan sponsor that can be detrimental to the retirement security of American workers and retirees. They can also serve to threaten the stability and credibility of the private pension system.

F. What type of activities am I speaking of? . . . I'm talking about actions by plan sponsors to terminate overfunded pension plans either to redeploy any surplus assets as a defensive measure or to pay for any takeover related debt in the case of a successful takeover. While these actions are legal, they are extremely troubling from a public policy perspective. There are, however, different approaches to addressing this matter, some of which would be inappropriate and counterproductive.

G. For example, Senator Proxmire, in his takeover-related legislation, proposes to take two steps that the Department, on behalf of the Administration, has gone on record as opposing. The first provision would amend section 404 of ERISA to state that, in considering a tender offer, "a fiduciary shall take into consideration the long-term as well as the short-term interests of the participants and beneficiaries." We feel this is inappropriate in that it would appear to set up a different standard for tender offers than for other plan management decisions. Whether it actually does or not is open to question; the Department's position has been that such fiduciary decisions be based on what is in the ultimate best economic interest of the plan over the period of time the asset is expected to be held. We feel strongly that this economic test is essential and that a level playing field for such decisions is appropriate. After all, while not all takeovers are good, not all are bad either. In addition, whether or not they're good is in the eyes of the beholder. In any event, the government is not in a position, nor would it be appropriate for it whether intentionally or not, to make this decision on a de facto basis through legislative fiat. Rather, it's only right to let the shareholders decide since they bear the investment risk. The second provision would preclude a successful acquirer from using any surplus assets in any pension plan to pay for any takeover debt. However, as we all know, money is fungible and, therefore, this rule is administratively infeasible. In addition, it does nothing to prevent plan terminations, which are of concern to the Department from a retirement policy perspective.

H. If Senator Proxmire's legislation is not the answer, then what is? The answer may lie in an important element to the Administration's Funding and Termination Proposal of February 1987 (for single employer defined benefit pension plans). Namely, additional restrictions on employer access to surplus assets on plan termination as compared with current law (i.e., aggregation concept, cushions above termination liabilities) and limited withdrawals from significantly overfunded pension plans, with appropriate protections to assure that benefit security is not compromised (e.g., cushions, frequency restrictions, valuation standards, etc.). This approach, which was not included in the Pension Protection Act that was part of the Budget Reconciliation Bill, has a number of benefits from a pension policy perspective, which I won't go into at this time, but it also has at least two from a takeover perspective. Namely, it would create a level playing field that would serve both as a "release valve" from a defensive perspective (i.e., by allowing access to a portion of any surplus assets for redeployment in the business) and as a "safety net" from an offensive vantage point (i.e., limiting how much surplus the successful acquirer could access). The result . . . improved benefit security, increased stability in the private pension system and within corporate America and, importantly, a decrease in the use of pension plans as pawns, which by being on the front line may be the first to fall prey in corporate takeover battles.

III. Overview of DOL actions

A. Given the growing importance of corporate governance (e.g., proxy voting) and related issues (e.g., takeovers) for ERISA plans and the significant potential for abuse (i.e., conflicting interests), the DOL has taken a number of definitive actions in this area since my last speech before the United Shareholders Association (USA) in June 1987 and will continue to do so as appropriate and necessary. For example:

1. I and several other Departmental officials have spoken out on numerous occasions and to a variety of groups regarding the importance of corporate governance and related issues and their ERISA implications. We have attempted to use the "bully pulpit" as a means of raising consciousness and the visibility of this issue and, as a result, providing additional assurance that the checks and balances in ERISA will work. This has been fruitful as evidenced by the growing amount of attention within the press and the ERISA community on these issues. At the same time, the "bully pulpit" alone is not enough, and the department has not and will not stop at that. We have also done the following.
2. Supported and contributed to various research initiatives dealing with corporate governance activities in order to obtain a better understanding of the various issues and the current state of affairs within the ERISA community.
3. Provided additional guidance regarding pass-through procedures in connection with tender offers via the Eastern/Texas Air litigation (11/87).
4. Former Secretary Brock sent a letter to Senator Proxmire stating the department's opposition to the ERISA-related provisions in his takeover bill. In this regard, the department will continue to monitor and comment on takeover-related legislation from an ERISA perspective as necessary and appropriate.
5. Identified the corporate governance area as in subset of our emphasis in institutional fiduciaries under our new enforcement strategy document (12/86). In this regard, several investigations are underway, one of which will result in a letter reinforcing the Department's position on various corporate governance matters. This letter will be available to the public and should receive a significant amount of attention in the press and the ERISA community once it is released. We expect the letter will be released within the next week, and it should, among other things, serve to remind plan fiduciaries of their ERISA

responsibilities and potential liability during the current and future proxy voting seasons. It will also serve as a tangible reminder that proxy voting by ERISA plans is a real issue for the Department with real potential consequences. After all, actions speak louder than words.

6. Finally, we will continue to coordinate with the SEC on proxy voting matters of mutual concern (e.g., one share/one vote, additional disclosure, secret ballot, independent tallies, etc.).

IV. Conclusion

In summary, while not all takeovers are good, not all proxy issues are either. In addition, it is clear that pension plans will play an ever-increasing role in proxy contests and takeover battles. In this regard, it is important that plan fiduciaries fully understand and properly discharge their responsibilities under ERISA. The Department will do its best to serve as an effective watchdog over these areas, but we can't do it all. We need the help of other interested parties as well. We will also continue to represent the interests of plan participants and beneficiaries in the important corporate governance and takeover areas. After all, it's critical that the retirement security of plan participants and beneficiaries not be subordinated to the interests of corporate management or any other parties. As most plan participants would say, "Don't mess with my pension; I earned it and I'm counting on it."

APPENDIX B

U.S. Department of Labor Letter of February 22, 1988, Describing the Procedural and Substantive Fiduciary Requirements Relating to Proxy Voting under ERISA

The Pension and Welfare Benefits Administration (PWBA) of the Department of Labor is responsible for administration and enforcement of Title I of the Employee Retirement Income Security Act of 1974 (ERISA). Title I establishes standards governing the operation of employee benefit plans and includes fiduciary responsibility rules governing the conduct of plan officials and others who exercise discretionary authority or control with respect to the assets of employee benefit plans, such as the Employees' Retirement Plan (the Plan), which are subject to ERISA.

PWBA has concluded its investigation of the Plan and of your activities as a fiduciary of the Plan, in connection with certain activities concerning the voting of proxies appurtenant to shares held in the accounts of the Plan's investment managers. The facts adduced during this investigation are not conclusive. However, because of the possibility that violations have occurred, and in view of the recurring nature of this aspect of plan asset management, we believe that it would be appropriate to apprise you of the Department's views concerning the general fiduciary obligations of a named fiduciary and an investment manager appointed pursuant to section 402(c)(3) of ERISA with respect to the voting of proxies on plan-owned stock. Since we expect that this information will be useful to the other members of the Plan's retirement board, and to the investment managers of the Plan, we are providing them with copies of this letter.

THE APPLICABLE PROVISIONS OF ERISA

Taken together, the provisions of ERISA sections 402, 403, 404, and 405 are intended to, among other things, provide a basis for certainty regarding the identity and responsibilities of those parties involved in managing and operating the plan, as well as each party's liability for mismanagement.

Section 402(a) of ERISA provides that every employee benefit plan shall be established and maintained pursuant to a written instrument. This instrument must provide for one or more named fiduciaries who have authority to control and manage the operation and administration of the plan. The named fiduciaries may be either named in the plan instrument or chosen, through a procedure specified in the plan, by the plan sponsor.

Section 402(b)(2) of ERISA requires plans to describe any procedure for allocating responsibilities for operation and administration of the plan, including any procedure described in section 405(c)(1).

Section 405(c)(1) of ERISA provides, in part, that the named fiduciaries may designate persons other than named fiduciaries to carry out fiduciary responsibilities (other than trustee responsibilities) under the plan. Section 405(c)(3) of ERISA defines *trustee responsibility* to mean any responsibility provided in the plan's trust instrument to manage or control the assets of the plan, other than a power under the trust instrument of a named fiduciary to appoint an investment manager in accordance with section 402(c)(3).

Section 403(a) of ERISA provides, in part, that all assets of an employee benefit plan must be held in trust by one or more trustees. The trustee(s) must have exclusive authority and discretion to manage and control such assets, with two exceptions: (1) when the plan expressly provides that the trustee(s) are subject to the direction of a named fiduciary who is not a trustee, in which case the trustees are subject to proper directions made in accordance with the terms of the plan and not contrary to ERISA, and (2) when the authority to manage, acquire or dispose of assets of the plan is delegated to one or more investment managers pursuant to section 402(c)(3).

Section 402(c)(3) of ERISA states that a plan may provide that with respect to control or management of plan assets a named fiduciary may appoint an investment manager or managers to manage (including the power to acquire and dispose of) plan assets.

Section 3(38) of ERISA defines *investment manager* as any fiduciary (other than a trustee or named fiduciary) (A) who has the power to manage, acquire, or dispose of any plan asset; (B) who is (1) a registered investment adviser under the Investment Advisers Act of 1940; (2) a bank; or (3) an insurance company; and (C) who has acknowledged in writing that he is a fiduciary with respect to the plan.

Section 405(c)(2) of ERISA provides, in part, that if a plan expressly provides for a procedure described in section 405(c)(1), and pursuant to such procedure a person is designated to carry out a fiduciary responsibility of a named fiduciary, then such named fiduciary shall not be liable for an act or omission of such person in carrying out such responsibility except to the extent that (A) the named fiduciary violated section 404(a)—(1) with respect to such designation, (2) with respect to the establishment or implementation of the procedure under 405(c)(1), or (3) in continuing the designation; or (B) the named fiduciary would otherwise be liable under ERISA section 405(a).

Section 404(a)(1)(B) of ERISA requires a fiduciary to discharge his duties to a plan with the care, skill, prudence, and diligence under the circumstances then prevailing that a prudent man acting in a like capacity and familiar with such matters would use in the conduct of an enterprise of a like character and with like aims.

Section 404(a)(1)(D) of ERISA requires a fiduciary to discharge his duties in accordance with the documents and instruments governing the plan insofar as such documents and instruments are consistent with the provisions of Titles I and IV of ERISA.

PROXY VOTING BY PLAN FIDUCIARIES

In general, the fiduciary act of managing plan assets that are shares of corporate stock would include the voting of proxies appurtenant to those shares of stock. For example, it is the Department's position that the decision as to how proxies should be voted with regard to the issues presented by the fact pattern are fiduciary acts of plan asset management: a proposal to change the state of incorporation of a corporation in which a plan owned shares (thereby possibly affecting shareholders' rights to participate in the decision-making process of the corporation which, in turn, affects the value of their investment) and a proposal to rescind "poison pill" arrangements with regard to various corporations in which a plan is invested. Moreover, because voting such proxies involves plan asset management, section 403(a) requires that plan trustees have the exclusive authority and responsibility for voting these proxies, unless one of the two exceptions stated in section 403(a) applies.

To the extent that the documents governing the plan permit a named fiduciary to appoint an investment manager pursuant to sections 402(c)(3) and 403(a)(2) of ERISA to manage, acquire, and dispose of plan assets, there would be an ERISA violation if, during the duration of such delegation, either the trustee or the named fiduciary makes the decision how to vote any proxy appurtenant to shares owned by the plan with respect to which the investment manager has investment authority because under the plan documents neither the trustee nor the named fiduciary has authority to make that decision with regard to those shares. Indeed, under such plan provisions if *any* person other than the investment manager (or a person under the fiduciary supervision of the investment manager)[1] were to make the proxy voting decision, there would be a section 404(a)(1)(D) violation because that person does not have that fiduciary authority under the plan. Finally, with limited exceptions,[2] the named fiduciary, having delegated such responsibility to the investment manager, no longer has the authority to decide how the investment manager votes proxies and would be engaging in a section 404(a)(1)(D) violation in doing so unless, in delegating such management responsibility to the investment manager, it reserves to itself the right to vote proxies.[3]

Moreover, ERISA contains no provision that would relieve an investment manager of fiduciary liability for any decision it made at the direction of another person. Under ERISA's construct, only trustees are able to relieve themselves of fiduciary responsibility and related liabilities by accepting directions, if plan documents so provide, and then only if such directions are "proper directions" made in accordance with the terms of the plan and not contrary to ERISA. Furthermore, neither section 3(38) nor 405(c) of ERISA grants an investment manager the powers of a named fiduciary to allocate or designate its investment management function for plan assets to other persons so as to relieve itself of its fiduciary responsibilities and related liabilities. Therefore, to the extent that anyone purports to direct an investment manager as to the voting of proxies, or to the extent that an investment manager purports to delegate to another the responsibility for such voting decisions,

---

[1] If the investment manager attempted to delegate his responsibility for proxy voting to another, the manager would not be relieved of his fiduciary responsibilities and related liabilities with regard to the voting decisions of that delegatee. (See discussion *infra*.)

[2] The general fiduciary responsibility provisions of ERISA, including the cofiduciary liability provisions, remain applicable to the named fiduciary's continuation of the delegation of asset management to the investment manager. Thus, no violation of section 404(a)(1)(D) would occur to the extent that ERISA's fiduciary responsibility provisions would require the named fiduciary to formally rescind the delegation to preclude the investment manager from engaging in a breach of fiduciary responsibility.

[3] To the extent that a named fiduciary reserves to itself the right to direct the trustee to vote proxies, the investment manager would not have fiduciary responsibility and related liability for the exercise of the vote. Moreover, to the extent the named fiduciary retains the voting rights, it would have full fiduciary responsibility and related liability for the exercise of those rights.

the manager would not be relieved of its own responsibilities and related liabilities merely because it either follows the direction of some other person, or has delegated the responsibility to some other person. The manager would continue to have full responsibility (and liability) for the exercise of the proxy voting decision.

Finally, the Department notes that section 404(a)(1)(B) requires the named fiduciary appointing the investment manager to periodically monitor the activities of the investment manager with respect to the management of plan assets. In general, this duty would encompass the monitoring of decisions made and actions taken by investment managers with regard to proxy voting. In this regard, it is the opinion of the Department that section 404(a)(1)(B) requires proper documentation of the activities of the investment manager and of the named fiduciary of the plan in monitoring the activities of the investment manager. Specifically, with respect to proxy voting, this would require the investment manager or other responsible fiduciary to keep accurate records as to the voting of proxies.[4]

We trust you will find the above information useful in discharging your ERISA responsibilities during the 1988 proxy season and thereafter.

Sincerely,

(Signed) Alan D. Lebowitz

Alan D. Lebowitz
Deputy Assistant Secretary

---

[4] Although this letter is concerned with the procedural requirements of ERISA as applied to proxy voting where an investment manager is appointed, the Department wishes to reiterate its longstanding interpretation of the substantive requirements of section 404(a)(1). Section 404(a)(1) requires, among other things, that a fiduciary of a plan act prudently, solely in the interest of the plan's participants and beneficiaries, and for the exclusive purpose of providing benefits to participants and beneficiaries. To act prudently in the voting of proxies (as well as in all other fiduciary matters), a plan fiduciary must consider those factors that would affect the value of the plan's investment. Similarly, the Department has construed the requirements that a fiduciary act solely in the interest of, and for the exclusive purpose of providing benefits to, participants and beneficiaries as prohibiting a fiduciary from subordinating the interests of participants, and beneficiaries in their retirement income to unrelated objectives.

APPENDIX C

U.S. Department of Labor Press Statement of May 11, 1988, Regarding a Limited Enforcement Review as a Follow-Up to the Department's Proxy Voting Guidance

David M. Walker, assistant secretary of the Pension and Welfare Benefits Administration of the Department of Labor, today announced the initiation of an enforcement project to monitor how investment managers with control over employee benefit plan assets subject to the Employee Retirement Income Security Act of 1974 (ERISA) are exercising their fiduciary responsibility in voting the stock owned by the plans whose assets they manage.

Specifically, the department through the Pension and Welfare Benefits Administration (PWBA) will determine how selected investment managers are exercising their responsibilities in light of the guidance provided by the department in this area.

Most recently, in February 1988, the department issued a letter in conjunction with an ERISA investigation that provided guidance on how proxy voting should be handled under ERISA. The letter addressed both procedural and substantive requirements, including, among other things, the requirement that such decisions must be made by the persons provided for in the plan document based on what is in the economic interest of the plan and viewing the plan as a separate legal entity established for the purpose of providing retirement income.

The department is currently reviewing data on recent major proxy issues as well as those financial institutions responsible for plan portfolios containing significant stock in those companies. The department plans to contact certain of those investment managers in the near future and will seek information on how the responsibility is allocated between the investment manager and other fiduciaries for voting proxies owned by the plan; whether and how the institution voted stock in the selected companies owned by the plans, including information about the internal decision-making process used by the manager; and the basis for the decision and appropriate documentation, including whether the investment manager acted on advice of another individual and the basis of such advice. Among other things, the department will examine those instances where an investment manager appears to be basing its decision with respect to the voting of proxies primarily on communications from an individual who has a personal or financial interest in the outcome of the vote and will pay particular attention to evidence of coercion by such person.

Assistant Secretary Walker stated, "This project is being undertaken to ensure that investment managers meet their responsibility as fiduciaries to properly vote stock owned by employee benefit plans. ERISA requires all investment managers to vote plan proxies solely in the best interest of plan participants and beneficiaries who, through their pension plans, are the beneficial owners of a significant and growing percentage of corporate America."

Recently, PWBA instituted a new enforcement strategy in which 50 percent of its investigative resources are devoted to two significant issues. One of these issues concerns management of pension fund assets by financial institutions, including investment managers, banks, insurance companies, and other financial institutions with discretionary authority over employee benefit pension plan assets. This project is both an outgrowth of the current PWBA enforcement strategy and a response to the important role that employee benefit plans play as major institutional investors and a growing interest in how corporate America is being governed. Employee benefit plans now own 24 percent of all equities in the United States. In addition, the department estimates that by the year 2000, employee benefit plans will own nearly 50 percent of all corporate equities in the United States.

The Pension and Welfare Benefits Administration is the agency within the Department of Labor responsible for enforcing the fiduciary and other provisions of Title I of the ERISA. ERISA requires plan fiduciaries, including investment managers, to act solely in the interest of a plan's participants and beneficiaries and with the care, skill, and prudence, under the circumstances, that a prudent man acting in a like capacity would use in the conduct of his own affairs.